前言

旅行指南系列《东京艺术之旅》，每册一个主题，带你从日本文化、艺术及设计的角度畅游东京。每册均有不同的艺术之旅顾问登场，本册以日本古董为主题。第一章的艺术之旅顾问是古伊万里瓷器研究专家、古董店老板伊万·特鲁塞尔。手纸社负责人、从事跳蚤市场策划及运营的北岛勋担任第二章的顾问。预约制茶寮经营者沟口实穗负责解读第三章。古布收藏家、经销商，经营 BORO note 品牌，也是活跃的作家的深山由美子是第四章的顾问。四位顾问在古董、古器物方面造诣极深，从各自的角度，提出了不同的东京古董游览方案，还有推荐的景点！在 22 个“日本古董专栏”中介绍了古董店及古董集市值得一看的古董，一定不要错过。

Introduction

TOKYO ARTRIP is a series of guidebooks about Tokyo. Each playful, walking spot introduced in each edition is selected from the perspective of Japanese culture, art & design. Several ARTRIP ADVISERS appear in each edition. In this book, *Japanese Antiques*, the following 4 ARTRIP ADVISERS appear: Yvon Trousselle, an antique expert and antique shop owner (PART 1); Isao Kitajima, a Tegamisha representative and flea market organizer (PART 2); Miho Mizoguchi, an organizer of a saryo which operates on an appointment system (PART 3); Yumiko Fukayama, an old fabric collector and a dealer as well as a writer with the name “BORO note” (PART 4). In this book, we take you to “playful, antique spots in Tokyo” recommended by these 4 experts of antiques and old things. Don’t forget to check 22 Japanese Antique Columns that give you hints of what to look for at antique shops and markets.

古董店 Dentsdelion 的内部景象（见第 12 页）
Some of the items in this picture are not available

目录

符号说明 ㊍营业时间 电 电话 休 休息日 费 入场费、门票 址 地址 交 交通路线 网 网站

※ 全部为含税价格。

※ 书中内容基于 2018 年 5 月信息。

CONTENTS

Icon Description (H) Hours of Operation (T) Telephone Number (C) Closed Days (F) Admission Fee (Ad) Address (Ac) Access (U) URL

※All prices include sales tax.

※All information contained in this book are as of May,2018.

第一章

历史悠久的日本古董

TRADITIONAL JAPANESE ANTIQUES

喜欢的事物对自己才有价值，比起知识，用自己的双眼甄别、选择更加重要

伊万出生于法国，在美国与古董结缘，在日本实现了梦想——开了一家古董店。伊万自己就是古伊万里瓷器的收藏家。“我的店里时常可以见到外国人的身影。他们多喜欢橱柜、屏风等大件物品，可以用于室内装饰。”但是，日本人大多喜欢器皿、坠子等小玩意，还有许多收藏家只钟情于某一类物件。“可能有人认为古董领域门槛很高。其实不具备专业知识也没有关系，有不懂的尽管问即可。重要的是，自己究竟是不是真心喜欢。器物上的瑕疵、缺口反而赋予了其独特之处。摒弃已有的刻板印象，不要先入为主，用心灵去感受，如果觉得喜欢，那便是所谓的邂逅了。”

The importan thing is to choose antiques based on what you like and what's valuable for you rather than based on knowledge

Yvan Trousselle was born in France, and became interested in antiques when he lived in the United States. He opened his dream antique shop in Japan. He is also a Ko-Imari (Imari ware in the Edo era) collector himself. He says, “I have many foreign customers and most of them purchase practical, large size furniture pieces such as tansu (chest) and byobu (folding screen). On the other hand, Japanese customers are often collectors of certain types of antiques and they prefer rather small items such as utsuwa (dinnerware/pottery) and netsuke (toggle on items hanging from kimono sash). Many people might think antiques are difficult to understand, but you don't need much knowledge of them. You can always ask questions, and you don't always need to agree with the answer. The important thing is not whether you believe the answer, but whether you like it. When you can find even damage and chips on the item charming without any knowledge and mindset, then that's the piece for you.”

ARTRIP ADVISER
艺术之旅顾问

伊万·特鲁塞尔
Yvan Trousselle

古伊万里瓷器研究专家。生于法国。20 多岁住在美国时，邂逅了日本的古董，开始收藏古伊万里瓷器。移居日本之后，2003 年，与妻子（日本人）共同开了一家古董店“Dentsdelion”。

Ko-Imari expert who was born in France and started collecting Ko-Imari after he became interested in Japanese antiques when he lived in the United States. After he moved to Japan, he opened an antique shop “Dentsdelion” with his Japanese wife in 2003.

古董集市

❶ 平和岛全国古董集市（平和岛）

在日本的室内古董集市中，平和岛全国古董集市的历史最为悠久。20 世纪 70 年代，上百家古董店铺，参加了在品川王子大饭店黄金厅举办的古董集市。自此，掀起了一股古董热潮，之后这个集市接连办了 170 多场，硕果累累，并赢得了消费者的信赖。近年，每次参加集市的店铺有近 300 家，近的来自东京都近郊，远的来自北海道、九州。一半以上的店铺从第一场至今一直参加。由此可见，人们对这一活动十分信任，其影响遍及全国。超过 450 平方米的会场中，陈列了几十万件古董。参加的店铺趁着这千载难逢的机会，争相展示自己引以为傲的藏品，其中不乏稀罕的古董。来这里的，不仅有古董迷，还有来采购的经销商。这是一个在古董中淘宝的绝佳机会，可以体验到一生仅有一次的邂逅所带来的喜悦。集会的最后一天从下午就开始收拾，所以来参加的话要趁早。

(时) 每年举办 5 次，10:00—17:00 (电) 03-3767-2141（仅举办期间可用）；03-5985-5101（非举办期间咨询用）(费) 免费 (址) 大田区平和岛 6-1-1 平和岛东京流通中心大楼 (交) 东京单轨电车流通中心站步行 1 分钟 (网) www.kottouichi.com

❶ HEIWAJIMA ANTIQUE FAIR (Heiwajima)

Heiwajima antique fair is the oldest among indoor antique fairs in Japan. It was held for the first time at Shinagawa Prince Hotel with 100 antique dealers in the midst of the 1970's antique craze in Japan. Since then, the fair has been held over 170 times and is recognized for its achievement and credibility. Around 300 antique dealers from Hokkaido to Kyushu are part of this fair as well as local dealers. More than half of them are original sellers, and that proves their level of credibility. It is quite a sight to see hundreds of thousands of antiques gathered all in one place over 4800 sq. ft. and since the sellers bring in their best quality items, antique fans and even dealers come to find rare items. The fair gives you a perfect opportunity to see a variety of antiques collected from all over Japan. You can surely find the perfect match for you. It is recommended to go early on the last day since the cleaning up starts in the afternoon.

(H) 5 times a year 10:00-17:00 (T) 03-3767-2141(during the fair), 03-5985-5101(outside the fair period) (F) Free Admission (Ad) Heiwajima Tokyo Ryutsu Center, 6-1-1 Heiwajima, Ota-ku (Ac) 1-min walk from Ryutsu Center Station (Tokyo Monorail) (U) www.kottouichi.com

❷ 古董店 Dentsdelion（秋叶原）

东京台东区鸟越的小菜横町商业街等区域，还保留着古老的昭和风情。这里有一家古董店叫作 Dentsdelion，沿用了传统的日式木结构房屋的风格。这一店铺的原型是 1957 年建于秋田的一家酒馆，尽管当时木材不足，但还是奢侈地保持原样从秋田移建了过来。天花板、楣窗上可看到漂亮的木材纹理，建筑本身极具观赏价值。店主伊万先生是一位古伊万里瓷器研究专家，店内摆放着他珍爱的古伊万里瓷器。瓷器的图案有“柿右卫门”采用赤绘手法绘制的、蓝色的“蓝柿”以及花魁、西洋景、动物等珍稀纹样。仅是看古伊万里瓷器的图案，就令人忘却了时间。除此之外，从印章盒等日常用品，到漆器、橱柜、佛像、屏风等高级藏品，店里的古董种类十分丰富。其中坠子、屏风没有摆放在店里，如果有意寻找，可直接询问。陈列在二楼的富有年代感的橱柜等古董，也值得一看。

㊐11:00—19:00 ㊓03-3837-1980 ㊡不定期休息 ㊕台东区台东 2-4-13 ㊌JR（日本铁路公司）东京地铁日比谷线秋叶原站、仲御徒町站步行 10 分钟 ㊔dontsdelion.com

❷ **Dentsdelion** (Akihabara)

"Dentsdelion" is an antique shop renovated from an old Japanese house. It is located in Torigoe, Taito-ku, an area filled with the nostalgic atmosphere of the Showa era. The building was originally built as a liquor store selling Akita-made products in 1957, and its construction used luxury lumber generously. From an architecture point of view, the ceiling board with beautiful wood grain and *ranma* (wooden ornamental transom) are also worth seeing. Inside the store, a large collection of Ko-Imari ware welcomes you. Watching "Kakiemon" style *Arita* ware with akae, "Ai-kakiemon" style using design in underglaze indigo blue, and exotic designs such as oiran, ijin, and animals, you will simply forget the time. The store offers a wide variety of antiques from reasonable *inban* (transferware) to luxury *shikki* (lacquerware), *makie* (lacquerware with gold leaf), tansu, *butsuzo* (buddha statues) and byobu. Just ask if you are looking for particular items since some are not displayed. There are more to see upstairs.

Ⓗ 11:00-19:00 Ⓣ 03-3837-1980 Ⓒ Irregular (Ad) 2-4-13, Taito, Taito-ku, Tokyo (Ac) 10-min walk from both Naka-Okachimachi Station (Tokyo Metro Line) and Akihabara Station (JR Line)
Ⓤ dentsdelion.com

二层除去了日式房屋的隔断，空间更加宽敞，摆满了古董、艺术品。仅收藏的橱柜，就包括药柜、衣柜以及船上使用的可叠放船柜等，尺寸多种多样。

The 2nd floor is even more exciting to explore. In a large open space, it's filled with antiques and art works. Only for the collection of tansu, there are a whole lot of varieties and sizes such as *kusuri-dansu* (medicine chest), *isho-dansu* (clothing-chest), and *funa-dansu* (ships chest).

直接沿用古老的日式居住空间布局是这家古董店的一大特点。店主能充分利用每一处空间，壁龛上装饰有挂轴、壶等，还运用楣窗、横木板等展出商品，因此来逛时一定不要错过任何一个角落。

The shop uses the structure of a traditional Japanese house very well. When you look carefully, you will find *tokonoma* (recess or alcove) with *kakejiku* (hanging scroll) and *tsubo* (vase) on display, as well as *ranma* and *nageshi* (beam) as interior decor.

天花板上悬吊着的灯也是在售商品。电灯一直保持通电状态，能够让人直接感受到它所营造的氛围。使用乳白色玻璃制造的具有日本大正时代风情的灯罩，种类十分丰富。

All the lightings hung on the ceiling are also for sale. Lights are already turned on, so it helps to see how they work in a room. There are also many choices for milk glass *dengasa* (lampshade) of Taisho-roman style.

店内还陈列有香盒，精致小巧，只有巴掌大小。许多香盒都蕴含了工匠的技术和巧思，有许多的设计灵感都来自动物，让人看到就不禁想要收藏。这些香盒也可以用作首饰盒。

These are palm-sized incense boxes called "*kogo*". High quality craftsmanship in details and fun designs such as animal motifs make them very collectible. They can also be used as accessory cases.

伊万里烧

伊万里烧指的是在日本佐贺县有田町生产的瓷器。因发货港口在伊万里，所以被称为伊万里烧。其中尤为著名的是“柿右卫门”种类的，产生于江户时代，在乳白色胎体上施以红色等颜色的彩绘。“柿右卫门”种类对麦森等 17 世纪欧洲瓷器的生产制造产生了巨大影响。在古董方面，一般认为江户时代的古伊万里瓷器最为著名，但其对产出年代的界定不是十分严格。

IMARI WARE

Imari is the general term of porcelain ware made in Arita town, Saga prefecture. It was named after Imari port where they were shipped from. “Kakiemon style”that puts enamel decoration on a white porcelain background orginated in the Edo era and it proved a major influence on porcelain making in Europe such as Meissen in the 17th century. Although Imari ware from the Edo era is called “Ko-Imari” and especially popular in antiques markets, there is no precise definition of the period.

坠子

日本江户时代，人们将坠子固定在和服腰带上，下端挂着烟草盒、印章盒等小物件。这样坠子可以防止小物件掉落。后来工匠逐渐在制作过程中加入了更多的奇思妙想，自此坠子成为男性的时尚饰品。坠子一般由象牙或黄杨等木材雕刻而成，多呈动物形象，有时也会雕刻成诙谐的形象，如今已经成为备受欢迎的美术品。已故的高圆宫宪仁亲王是为大家所熟知的坠子收藏家，在上野公园北端的东京国立博物馆还设有高圆宫收藏室。

NETSUKE

Netsuke was a practical item in the Edo era that acted as a toggle on *sagemono* (hanging objects) such as tobacco pouches and *inros* (a small lacquered box) hung beneath kimono sashes to avoid falling. As craftsmen started to be more creative and make design variations, netsuke became a men's fashion item. These animal figures and humorous motifs made of wood such as boxwood and ivory are also popular as art pieces. The late Prince Takamado was a known netsuke collector and his collection can be seen at Tokyo National Museum.

❸ 古美术品店西川（麻布十番）

古美术品店西川创立于明治时代，总店位于日本滋贺县长浜市，本书介绍的是其东京店。据店铺第三代经营者西川英树介绍，在开店的 40 年前，原本被称为日本“大陆孤岛”的麻布十番建起车站，交通更加便利，街区日渐繁荣。如今的麻布十番，老牌饮食店铺鳞次栉比，街区虽然繁华，但仍然给人以静谧的感觉。这里有许多古董店，还有各国大使馆，因此店铺里经常能见到外国客人的身影。店内有一块仿照茶室打造的区域，摆放着许多屏风以及摆件。器物占据了店铺一半的空间，其中包括古伊万里及九谷烧等瓷器。“日本料理被列为世界非物质文化遗产之后，日本掀起了一股料理热潮，无论是日料店还是普通家庭，都开始在餐具上花费心思。哪怕只有一件古董餐具，整个餐桌都会瞬间变得有格调。”无论是华美的古伊万里瓷器，还是简约的青花瓷，都会使日常的餐桌变得典雅高贵。逐渐集齐喜欢的花纹，也不失为一种乐趣。

㊐11:00—18:00 ㊉03-3456-1023 ㊡星期二 ㊟港区麻布十番 2-20-14 ㊛地铁麻布十里站步行 5 分钟 ㊠www.nishikawa.to

❸ Nishikawa Antiques (Azabu-juban)

A Tokyo branch of Nishikawa Antiques in Nagahama, Saga, established in the Meiji era. Nishikawa (3rd owner) says, "After the train station was made, Azabu-juban became a quite vibrant town compared to 40 years ago." The area is popular among tourists because of its vibrant yet relaxing atmosphere, filled with antique shops and long-established restaurants. The shop also gets many foreign customers because of different countries'embassies in the area. In the shop, you see a small space imitating a tea room, various okimono (ornaments) and byobu. Half of the shop is filled with utsuwa such as Ko-Imari and Kutani. The owner says, "Since Japanese cuisine became popular after being added to UNESCO's Intangible Cultural Heritage list, Japanese tableware also gained recognition among not only restaurants but also the general public. One antique piece can add a flavor to the table." Gorgeous Ko-Imari and chic *sometsuke* take daily food to another level. Buying one piece at a time is also fun.

(H)11:00-18:00 (T)03-3456-1023 (C)Tuesday (Ad)2-20-14 Azabu-juban, Minato-ku (Ac)5-min walk from Azabu-juban Station (Toei Line) (U)www.nishikawa.to

は御座いますのでお尋ね下さい。
We have more stock.

一整面墙都摆满了古伊万里瓷器。古伊万里瓷器不仅可以用来盛放日本料理，与意大利料理、少数民族特色料理也十分契合。接待客人时一般会摆放同样花纹的餐具，但使用各不相同花纹的也会很和谐。

A wall of Ko-Imari ware. Ko-Imari goes well with not only Japanese food but also Italian and ethnic foods. Having a set of the same design tableware for entertaining guests is a good idea but combining different patterns and colors is also fun and creates a nice unison.

❹ 古美术品专卖店长谷部屋（麻布十番）

拥有 40 年历史的长谷部屋坐落于麻布十番商业街的一角，对面是著名的鲷鱼烧（一种日式点心）店和煎饼店。店主长谷部纯一十分喜欢古董，大学毕业后开了这家店，现在儿子长谷部智信与他一同经营。店铺中除日本古董之外，还会出售韩国和中国的古董。店铺共两层，古美术品被店主按照相同间隔摆放开来，走进店铺中仿佛走进了美术馆。与美术馆不同的是，在这里可以将喜欢的古董拿在手中观看，还可以直接购买带走。长谷部纯一介绍，以前也流行收藏古董以及古美术品，但是现在更加多元化。人们不再根据领域来挑选，而是根据自己的喜好来选择。因此，店里的器物种类十分丰富。酒具、人偶、多层橱柜、阿伊努族（日本北方的一个原住民族群）的和服、神乐面具、玻璃彩绘等，看似种类繁杂，但是整体和谐统一，因为这些器物都是上乘的佳品，都具有相同的空灵质感。来到这里，一定可以找到喜欢的器物，也正因为如此，这里受到了许多外国收藏家的青睐。

(时)11:00—18:00 (电)03-5775-1308 (休)休息日不定 (址)港区麻布十番 1-7-7 (交)地铁麻布十番站步行 3 分钟 (网)无

❹ **Hasebeya** (Azabu-juban)

Hasebeya, a 40-year-old antique shop, is at the corner of a shopping arcade facing popular *taiyaki* (fish-shaped cake) and *senbei* (Japanese rice cracker) shops. Junichi Hasebeya opened the shop after graduating from college. Now his son Tomonobu joins the business and they sell Korean and Chinese antiques as well. Inside the 2-storey shop, you will see art works displayed regularly like a museum. The difference is you can touch and buy them. The owner says, "Antiques used to have waves of a popular genre, but now people choose antiques based on their tastes. To suit versatile tastes, we offer a variety of things." Here, you see *shuki* (sake serving set), *ningyo* (doll), *kaidan-dansu* (staircase chest), *Ainu* kimono, mask of *kagura* (Shinto music and dance) and *garasu-e* (reverse glass painting). Each of them is unique, yet they give a harmonious look because of their similar feeling and quality. The shop is also well known among overseas collectors for finding something nice.

Ⓗ 11:00-18:00 Ⓣ 03-5775-1308 Ⓒ Irregular (Ad) 1-7-7 Azabu-juban, Minato-ku (Ac) 3-min walk from Azabu-juban Station (Toei Line) Ⓤ N/A

刚一走进门，就可以看到一片展区。多层橱柜和设计大气的壶等，都可以成为布置房间的亮点。该展区的重点是阿伊努族的服装，由斜向袖子的设计，可推测这件衣服是女性服装。

Here is a display section at the entrance area with accent furniture such as kaidan-dansu and large vases. On the wall is an Ainu costume. Sleeves in a diagonal line are a typical design for female costumes.

髭皿

髭皿边缘有一个半月形的缺口，17 至 19 世纪出口到欧洲，作为理发店剃胡须时专用：将半月状缺口紧贴脖子，便于收集被剃下的胡须。半月状缺口的另一边有两个孔，是为了方便理发师挂在腰上，也可挂在墙壁上作为装饰。伊万里烧等纹样华美的器物在江户时代中期通过荷兰东印度公司出口到欧洲，在欧洲受到欢迎。

HIGEZARA

Higezara (shaving bowl) is a shallow bowl with a semi-circle cutout along the edge to place against customers' necks to collect shaved facial hair. There are two holes facing the semi-circle for the barber to hang from his waist. It's also good as a decoration on the wall. The shaving bowl was made to import to Europe for barbers from the 17th to the 19th century. It was imported to Europe by the Dutch East India Company. Beautiful Imari designs were particularly popular.

花篮

用竹子精心编织成的花篮是日本代表性的传统工艺品。如今，跨越了传统工艺的界限，花篮在古董、美术品领域也备受关注。正如其名，花篮是用来插花的装饰品，而一些设计精美的花篮作为艺术品在其他国家也极受欢迎，在巴黎的美术馆甚至还举办过相关展览。日本的竹艺技术在世界上是首屈一指的，其精湛的工艺在岁月流逝中仍然魅力不减。

HANAKAGO

Hanakago, a flower basket made of delicately woven bamboo, is one of the Japanese traditional craftworks. They are also recognized as antique and art pieces beyond a genre of craftwork. Hanakago literally means an ornamental vase basket to put flowers in. However, some are particularly popular overseas for their decorative designs as art objects. Even an exhibition was held at a gallery in Paris. Japanese *bamboo craft* skill is the world's best, and the beauty of delicate and meticulous craftsmanship is timeless.

❺ 灯屋（参宫桥）

1981 年（昭和五十六年），当时只有 29 岁的涩谷新三郎，就自己开了一家古董店。他想，一定有人喜欢在生活中享受古器物的美，但是他们又不懂怎样去选择，需要的是为他们照亮路途的一盏灯，所以他为店铺起名“灯屋”。36 年过去了，现在涩谷先生还会在法国的美术馆举办花篮、竹工艺的主题展览，在海外也点亮了一盏灯。涩谷先生喜欢手工制作的物品，他收藏的古董，每一件都把日本手工艺的精湛技艺和无上美感展现得淋漓尽致。涩谷先生希望大家用两只眼睛去欣赏——“一只眼睛是感官和感性，另一只眼睛是分析之后进行思考。如果觉得美丽，觉得喜欢，就要观察它的美感来自哪里。深入鉴赏，深入解析自己的兴趣爱好，充满着无限趣味。”鉴赏古董，可以找到自己的兴趣，遇见一个崭新的自己。

(时) 11:00—19:00 (电) 03-3465-5578 (休) 星期日、节假日 (址) 涩谷区代代木 4-8-1 (交) 小田急线参宫桥站步行 5 分钟 (网) www.akariya.co.jp

❺ AKARIYA (Sangubashi)

The owner, Shibutani, opened his shop in 1981 at the age of 29. He named it "Akariya" aiming to be the small light to guide people who may feel lost in the dark when it comes to judging antiques. Since then, Akariya has been the light for customers from Japan and overseas for 36 years. The shop held a hanakago and bamboo craft theme exhibition in a museum in France. Shibutani says, "I especially admire hand crafted items." The antiques he collects are the Japanese craftsmanship pinnacle of quality and beauty. He also says, "I'd like people to look at antiques with both eyes. First, with one eye, you would see antiques with your senses, then with the other eye, you would think and analyze them. When you see interesting or beautiful things, you should observe carefully and find out why you think that way. I'd like you to experience the fun of analyzing things closely. "By observing antiques, you discover an interest and find a new you as well.

Ⓗ 11:00-19:00 Ⓣ 03-3465-5578 Ⓒ Sunday and National Holidays (Ad) 4-8-1 Yoyogi, Shibuya-ku
(Ac) 5-min walk from Sangubashi Station (Odakyu Line) Ⓤ www.akariya.co.jp

❻ 古玩店 TORITORI（西荻洼）

东京 23 区最西端的街区西荻洼，是一条古董古玩街。第二次世界大战之前，一部分商人购买了附近大户人家留传下来的器物，放在古器物店内售卖，这便是这条古玩街的起源。现在，这一带共有 60 多家古器物店铺，每年在春季和秋季各举办一次“西荻古董节”。TORITORI 就开在西荻洼，已有 22 年的历史，店内出售的商品具有女性独有的风格。店主野口知子女士自身也是一位古董收藏家，对精美可爱的器物爱不释手。过家家的迷你玩具、贴花日式布艺品、赛璐珞人偶和文具、簪子、串珠包等，小小的店面中摆满了可爱的小物件，宛若一个玩具箱。每年春天店铺会举办“TORITORI 女儿节”，展示各式各样的小人偶、小玩具、迷你手工艺品等，绝对值得一看。许多游客为了得到平时罕见的小玩具，每年都千里迢迢赶来参加。

(时) 12:00—18:00 (电) 03-5382-8409 (休) 休息日不定 (址) 杉并区西荻北 4-5-24 白亚公寓 1 层 (交) JR 西荻洼站步行 5 分钟 (网) ameblo.jp/toritori-nishiogi

❻ TORITORI (Nishiogikubo)

Nishi-Ogikubo, located in the westernmost point of Tokyo's 23 wards, is an antique town. It all started when the number of *furudogu-ya* (shops of second-hand articles) increased to sell unwanted second-hand articles coming from mansions in the area before WWII. Now there are more than 60 shops selling old things and the town also hosts the biannual NISHIOGI ANTIQUE FESTIVAL in spring and fall. In a 22-year-old antique shop *TORITORI*, there is a hint of a feminine touch in its merchandise selections. The owner, Noguchi is an antique collector herself and has a weakness for cute things. Her small shop is like a toy box filled with things such as miniature toys for playing house, *oshie-zaiku* (textile painting), celluloid dolls and stationaries, *kanzashi* (ornamental hair pin)and beaded bags. "TORITORI *Hina-Matsuri* (Doll Festival)" is held every spring and is a must-see event where you can find collections of hina dolls, hina goods and miniature hina handcrafts. Many people come from far away every year to buy rare collectibles.

Ⓗ 12:00-18:00 Ⓣ 03-5382-8409 Ⓒ Irregular (Ad) 4-5-24 Nishiogi Kita, Suginami-ku (Ac) 5-min walk from Nishi Ogikubo Station (JR Line) Ⓤ ameblo.jp/toritori-nishiogi

Flâneur

独具匠心的手工艺品、工艺繁杂的迷你工艺品等，店内聚集了众多日本古代的精湛的手工艺品。店铺外面也摆放着商品。在这里，你可以充分感受到从遇见到喜欢，再到收藏一件古董的快乐。

Inside the shop, you can see it's filled with items crafted with elaborate designs and intricate miniature hina dolls which remind us of Japanese craftsmanship of the good old days. Merchandise is also displayed outside the store. Collecting is another way to enjoy antiques, and here at TORITORI, you can enjoy just looking at antiques and it becomes even more satisfying by collecting them.

佛像

佛像作为信仰和崇拜的对象被制作出来，是为了传播佛教的思想。佛像传到日本是在飞鸟时代，公元 538 年左右。除了有释迦牟尼像之外，还有以如来、菩萨、明王、天部、罗汉、佛弟子、高僧等为造型的佛像，这些佛像一大特点是通过表情和服饰来表现人物形象。佛像作为佛教美术品和古美术品，均受到人们的极高评价，著名工匠制作的佛像还会被作为艺术品用于交易，甚至还有专门收藏佛像的收藏家。

BUTSUZO

Butsuzo (Buddha statues) were produced as objects of faith to worship and to preach Buddhism. It is said that butsuzo appeared in Japan around 538 AD. These statues have categories based on rankings which are, from the top, *Shaka*, *Nyorai*, *Bosatsu*, *Myo-o*, *Ten*, *Rakan*, *Butsudeshi*, and *Ko-so*. Their facial expressions and costumes reflect different characteristics of each category. Butsuzo are well recognized as articles of Buddhist art and antiquities. Works of famous *busshi* are considered art pieces and extremely popular among collectors.

时代橱柜

日式橱柜也被称作时代橱柜，种类颇多，包括装衣物的衣柜、材质坚硬用于船上的叠放式船柜、盛放账本的账本柜、底部装有轮子的手推橱柜、可做楼梯使用的楼梯式橱柜、用于厨房的水池柜和用于茶室的茶柜等。这种橱柜是在榉树上涂漆，再安装上金属零件制成的。在室内装修中如果加入这样一个橱柜，可以增加一抹厚重感。

JIDAIDANSU

Wadansu (traditional Japanese chest), also known as *jidai-dansu*, include robust *funa-dansu* (ships chest), *choba-dansu* used to store accounting books, *kuruma-dansu* which comes with small wheels, *kaidan-dansu* (stair case chest) used as real stairs, *mizuya-dansu* used in a bathroom and kitchen area, and *cha-dansu* used in a tea house. These dansu made of lacquered Zelkova tree with metallic decoration give a profound feeling to the overall interior decors.

❼ 银座古玩商场（银座）

银座古玩商场是亚洲最大的古董专门购物中心，除日式古董店之外，还汇集了和服、古布、西方古董等各式各样的店铺。商场负责人中村美雪还协助东京国际展览中心共同举办了“古董狂欢节”。翻新之后的银座古玩商场，第一层有出售日本古董及其他亚洲古董的店铺，总面积达 200 平方米，地下是各式各样的古董店铺，一次可以逛许多家。每家店铺出售的商品也会时常更新，有华美的复古风格和服、日式古器物（比如茶具）及古美术品等，最好在逛完一圈之后选择自己喜欢的店铺，并在之后持续关注。商场有一层楼专门设置展示柜，展示了 80 多家商店的商品，绝对值得一看。除了经销商之外，个人也可以委托代售商品，无数量限制，1 件也可以。所以在这里还可以遇到此前一直被“雪藏”在家里或收藏家个人出售的珍品。银座古玩商场还经常举办展览以及室内活动等，在网站上可以获取相关信息。

㊐11:00—19:00 ㊑03-3535-2115 ㊡全年无休 ㊒中央区银座 1-13-1 ㊓东京地铁有乐町线银座一丁目站步行 2 分钟 ㊔www.antiques-jp.com

❼ Antique Mall Ginza (Ginza)

Antique Mall Ginza is the largest antique-only shopping mall in Asia where a variety of shops selling Japanese antiques, kimono and old fabrics, and Western antiques all come together. Nakamura, the representative, also co-hosts "The Antique Jamboree" at Tokyo Big Site every year. The mall has been renewed recently and in a 2150 sq. ft. space on the 1st floor, a brand new shop of Japanese and Asian antiques just opened. In the basement, there are antique shops of various genres, so you can go around from one shop to another. Since each one sells some specific antique genre such as cute vintage kimono, old Japanese utsuwa, tea ceremony utensils and old works of art, we recommend you to walk around first, and come back to a shop you would like to spend more time at. In particular, the "Case Floor" where more than 80 dealers showcase their items is a must-see. Since some cases are for consignment that anybody can sell from 1 item, you may find rare and unexpected item among individual collections. Please check the official web site for fairs and special events.

Ⓗ11:00-19:00 Ⓣ03-3535-2115 Ⓒ None (Ad)1-13-1 Ginza, Chuo-ku (Ac) 2-min-walk from Ginza 1-chome Station (Tokyo Metro Line) Ⓤ www.antiques-jp.com

到伊万里烧收藏家聚集地——户栗美术馆看一看

TO THE MUSEUM OF POTTERY AND PORCELAIN, A MEETING POINT FOR IMARI-COLLECTORS

户栗美术馆创立于 1987 年，位于东京涩谷区松涛，原本是日本锅岛家族的住宅遗址。户栗美术馆是日本为数不多的陶瓷专业美术馆之一，展示的是该美术馆创始人户栗亨多年以来收藏的陶瓷。展品包括伊万里烧、锅岛烧等日本肥前地区的陶瓷以及产自中国、朝鲜的东方陶瓷 7000 件左右。馆内还提供有《陶瓷展览解说入门》，介绍了伊万里烧的历史及鉴赏方法和展览相关信息。馆内还有专业职员开设的讲座(需要预约、收费)。在这里，即使不了解陶瓷器，也可以深入展览，收获快乐。

Toguri Museum of Art opened at the former site of Nabeshima family residence in Shoto, Shibuya-ku in 1987. It is one of the few museums specializing in pottery and porcelain in Japan. It exhibits the pottery and porcelain collection of the founder Toru Toguri, and around 7, 000 Oriental pottery and porcelain from China and Korea as well as Hizen porcelain (Imari and Nabeshima) ware owned by the museum. A guided tour with an introduction class for pottery and curator's lecture on the exhibition (reservation & fee required) are also available to understand the exhibition better.

户栗美术馆（涩谷）

(时) 10:00—17:00（星期五 20:00 闭馆）(电) 03-3465-0070 (休) 星期一（每月第四个星期一正常营业）、元旦假期、展览更换期间 (费) 1 000 日元（1 日元 ≈0.06 人民币）(址) 涩谷区松涛 1-11-3 (交) 涩谷站步行 15 分钟，京王井头线神泉站步行 10 分钟 (网) www.toguri-museum.or.jp

TOGURI MUSEUM OF ART (Shibuya)

(H) 10:00-17:00 (Fri -20:00) (T) 03-3465-0070 (C) Mondays (except every 4th Monday of month), New Year's Holiday and Change up period (F) ¥1,000 (Ad) 1-11-3 Shoto, Shibuya-ku (Ac) 15-min walk from Shibuya Station (JR Line), 10-min walk from Shinsen Station (Keio Line) (U) www.toguri-museum.or.jp

美术馆的标志是以伊万里烧青花瓷“竹虎纹拈花盘”上的老虎为原型进行设计的。据说是因为美术馆创始人户栗氏出生于虎年，因此十分喜欢绘有老虎花纹的陶瓷。馆内也陈列了许多老虎纹的盘子，参观时可以找找看。

The Museum’s logo mark is a tiger, the motif painted in Imari ware “sometsuke-taketoramon-nejibana-plate” simply because the museum founder was born in the year of the tiger and loved pottery with tiger motifs. Many tiger motif plates are seen in the museum.

美术馆每年举办 4 次展览，每次设定一个主题，从大量的藏品中选定一部分进行展示。与此同时，还会在瓷器陈列室中举办与展览主题相符的现代瓷器艺术家的个展及收藏陶片的小型展览。每次到来都会有新发现。

Every year, the museum opens 4 special exhibitions with different themes. It also hosts private shows in the pottery room by modern porcelain artists and mini potsherd display related to the special exhibitions, so the museum always offers something new to discover.

馆内还设有休息区，可以在沙发上小憩。在饮品区还可以购买咖啡等饮品，一边品尝咖啡，一边欣赏庭院的风景，就会不由得忘却时间。在休息区还可以浏览过去展览的资料及展板等。

The museum has a lounge space where you can relax and enjoy the garden view through the four seasons. Visitors can also check archived references and description panels of the past exhibitions at the lounge. There are soft drinks available to purchase.

面具

面具分为狂言面具和能乐面具。狂言面具的创作题材是平民的喜剧，能乐面具的创作题材是贵族的悲剧，二者在创作主题及人物表情上均有差异。狂言面具大多是根据鬼、福神、老人、丑女、动物等进行创作，表情独特。而能乐面具的种类则有老翁、年轻女子、鬼神、恶魔等，其中年轻女子的最大的特点是看起来既像是在笑，又像是在哭。这些面具展示的形象可以使人联想到其中的故事情节，十分有趣。

MASK

There are Kyogen and Noh masks. Based on different themes between Kyogen and Noh, their expressions are also different. Kyogen masks often give humorous expressions of characters such as gods, evil spirits, old men, *fukunokami*, ugly women, and animals. Noh masks, also known as *omote* portrait characters such as *okina*, female, fierce deity and vengeful spirit, and its female mask has a very subtle expression which looks like smiling and crying at the same time. In a way, these masks can tell you the story.

刀护手

日本刀在全世界拥有众多收藏家，刀的护手、孔钉等组成部件也十分受欢迎。护手位于刀柄或剑柄与刀身之间，是用来保护手的圆形配件，非常实用。自江户时代起，护手开始起到装饰作用。有的护手是在铁、铜的原材料上点缀上金色，有的护手呈现精巧的方形设计、镂空花纹等，从中可感受到工匠的匠心。若想亲眼欣赏刀护手，可以去东京的刀剑博物馆或东京国立博物馆。

TSUBA OF KATANA

Besides katana, that are already a very popular item among collectors worldwide, its accessories are also popular such as *tsuba* (a sword guard) and *menuki* (a hilt ornament). Tsuba is a round-shaped part that sits between the blade and grip and protects hands from the blade. It served to be practical and later became more decorative since the Edo era. Some are gold plated over iron and copper, square shaped or come with fretwork design. You can see them at the Japanese Sword Museum and Tokyo National Museum,both in Tokyo.

第二章

融入日常生活的古器物

OLD ARTICLES FIT
A PRESENT DAILY LIFE

与现代生活同样契合，上乘的材质和巧妙的设计惹人注目

日本手纸社主要举办东京跳蚤市场、布博览会、纸博览会等展览活动，汇集日本各地的店铺及品牌。手纸社的北岛勋先生介绍：“开始举办活动之前，我们会去逛各个古董集市，去的次数多了，认识了一些一直参加集市的店主，他们非常有经验，特别开心。”北岛勋先生非常喜欢年长和年轻的店主都参加的古董集市。手纸社运营的店铺在东京共有 5 家，店内的装修就使用了日本的古器物。“像灯、书架，还有门窗，用了好多日本的古器物。这些古器物都非常引人注目，将其摆放在关键位置时会使空间重点突出并且协调统一。这些古器物的制作工艺以及材质都属上乘。”

Old articles that also match modern life attract people with their high quality materials and elaborate designs

“Tokyo Nominoichi”, “nuno-haku (fabric exposition)” and “kami-haku (paper expo)” are events organized by Tegamisha assembling specially selected shops nationwide. Isao Kitajima of Tegamisha said, “I visited many antique markets before organizing these events and enjoyed meeting experienced shop owners such as the doyen of each market.” He particularly likes antique markets joined by both experienced and young shop owners. There are five shops run by Tegamisha in Tokyo, and Japanese second-hand articles are used as their interiors. Kitajima said, “We use mostly old Japanese lightings, bookshelves and fittings. I feel that they create a tense atmosphere when used in key areas because of their strong presence. The excellent workmanship and materials fascinates me.”

ARTRIP ADVISER
艺术之旅顾问

北岛勋
Isao Kitajima

日本手纸社负责人，主办东京跳蚤市场、布博览会等活动，还经营书店、杂货铺、咖啡店等。除手纸社踯躅丘总店、手纸社 2nd Story 店之外，在东京共有 5 家店铺，同时在镰仓和中国台湾也开有店铺。

Representative of Tegamisha who organizes “Tokyo Nomino-ichi”, “nuno-haku” and many other events. In Tokyo he runs 5 shops including the main store selling books and accessories with a café space. Other shops are in Kamakura and Taiwan.

❽ 大江户古董集市（有乐町、原宿）

大江户古董集市是日本规模最大的室外古董集市，举办地点为有乐町东京国际会议中心以及原宿的代代木公园榉树大道。2003 年，为纪念江户幕府建立 400 周年，以“重新审视日本古器物之美，再发掘日本文化”为主题，这两地举办了第一届大江户古董集市。现在大江户古董集市已经成为定期举办的人气古董集市，并被确立为一个交流文化与艺术、结识不同国家和不同年龄层朋友的平台。在东京国际会议中心举办的集市约有 250 家店铺参加，代代木公园榉树大道的集市约有 180 家店铺参加，展示出的商品除日式古董外，还有丰富的西方古玩、旧杂货。集市上聚集了来自世界各地的珍稀古董以及独特的旧杂货、玩具等，景象甚为壮观。商品的展示方式多种多样，仅是观看就已是一种享受。有许多年轻的店主和没有实体店的商户也来参加，在这里可以淘到许多难得一遇的珍品。

(时)东京国际会议中心是每月第 1 个和第 3 个星期日，代代木公园榉树大道举办时间不定。开放时间为 9:00—16:00 (电)03-6407-6011（从举办前一天傍晚开始提供服务）(费)免费 (址)千代田区丸之内 3-5-1 东京国际会议中心地面广场；涩谷区神南 2 代代木公园榉树大道 (交)东京国际会议中心：JR 有乐町站步行 1 分钟。代代木公园榉树大道：JR 原宿站步行 5 分钟 (网)www.antique-market.jp

❽ Oedo Antique Market
(Yurakucho · Harajuku)

Oedo Antique Market was launched in 2003 to celebrate the 400th anniversary of the founding of Edo as the largest outdoor one in Japan held at Tokyo Int'l Forum in Yurakucho and Yoyogi Park Keyaki-Namiki in Harajyuku. "Rediscover Japanese culture by re-examining the value of good old things" was the theme. It has become very popular and settled as a place to exchange culture and art and meet people of different ages and nationalities. The stalls in Tokyo Int'l Forum and Yoyogi Park Keyaki-Namiki are 250 and 180 respectively, filled with Japanese and Western antiques and brocantes. It's spectacular to see the market filled with valuable antiques from home and abroad and unique odds and ends and toys. Just watching the unique displays is fun. Many stall holders are young shop owners and non-shop owners, and there are many distinctive items available only here.

(H) Tokyo Int'l Forum: Every 1st&3rd Sunday. Yoyogi Park Keyaki-Namiki: Irregular. Both are 9:00-16:00 (T) 03-6407-6011 (From evening the day before the event day) (F) Free (Ad) Tokyo Int'l Forum: Plaza, 3-5-1 Marunouchi, Chiyoda-ku. Yoyogi Park Keyaki-Namiki: 2 Jinnan, Shibuya-ku. (Ac) Tokyo Int'l Forum: 1-min walk from Yurakucho Station (JR Line). Yoyogi Park Keyaki-Namiki: 5-min walk from Harajuku Station (JR Line) (U) www.antique-market.jp

¥4000.
トレー

在东京国际会议中心现代化的建筑空间内，来自全球各地，源于不同时代的古董古玩汇聚于此，看起来十分有趣。在银座这个熙熙攘攘的购物中心，不同的时代、文化、国籍的东西得到了有机的融合，这也恰好符合东京的国际化特色。

It's fun to see that Japanese and Western antiques are displayed together in contrast with the modern architecture of Tokyo international Forum. You can enjoy a typical Tokyo style market since different eras, cultures and nationalities are mixed at the popular shopping area of Ginza.

❾ 东京跳蚤市场（调布）

东京跳蚤市场聚集了来自日本各地的二手物品店、古玩店、杂货店和手工艺品店等，数量超过 230 家。到 2017 年为止共举办了 12 届，每年有许多人不远万里赶来参加。在这里不仅可以享受到购买日式古董、古玩等的乐趣，还可以一整天免费体验手工制作，欣赏演奏家的现场演出。另外，饮食区有许多售卖食物的摊铺，但是要做好排队的心理准备。还有售卖自制啤酒、咖啡等饮品的摊铺，在搜寻古器物疲劳之余可以在这里小憩。只有东京跳蚤市场才能聚集如此多平时很难逛到的各地的古董店。还有许多人带孩子一起来，这也已经成为家庭共同参与的一项活动。不仅在东京，在其他地方也会举办类似集市，如关西跳蚤市场、东海跳蚤市场，均受到好评。

㊐ 每年 5 月、11 月举办，9:00—17:00 ㊉ 042 444-5367（手纸社）㊊ 500 日元（小学生及以下年龄人群免费）㊋ 调布市多摩川 4-31-1 东京京王阁竞轮场 ㊌ 京王相模原线京王多摩川站步行 1 分钟 ㊍ tokyonominoichi.com

❾ Tokyo Nominoichi (Chōfu)

More than 230 shops of second-hand articles, antiques, accessories and handicraft brands are assembled at Tokyo Nominoichi. The 12th exhibition was held in 2017 and visited by many people looking forward to it every year even coming from far away. It's a good event to enjoy shopping for wakotto, antiques and antique books and to participate in workshops and free live performances by famous artists all day long. Many food stands are lined up, but be ready to make a long line. Many types of drinks such as home-made ones, craft beer and coffee will give you comfort when tired after looking for antiques. Tokyo Nominoichi is the only market that assembles such a large number of popular local shops that we can hardly visit at ordinary times. Nominoichi has become popular in Tokyo as an event that the whole family (including small children) can enjoy and has been held at other areas such as "Kansai Nominoichi" and "Tokai Nomonoichi" with a good reputation.

Ⓗ May and Nov. every year 9:00-17:00 Ⓣ 042-444-5367 (Tegamisha) Ⓕ 500yen (Free elementary school student or under) (Ad) Tokyo Oval Keiokaku, 4-31-1 Tamagawa Chofu (Ac) 1-min walk from Keio Tamagawa Station (Keio Line) Ⓤ tokyonominoichi.com

每一个摊位展出的商品都体现了店主的审美和店铺的特色，因此如果遇到吸引自己的商品，可能说明你和店主的兴趣相仿。细细品鉴，找到自己喜欢的物品吧。

Articles in the booths reflect the shop owner's sense of selection and their personality. If you find a favorite article in a shop, you may probably share the same sense as the shop owner. Take a careful look and find your favorite things.

展出商品中还有纽扣、串珠、线圈等手工用品。纽扣大多是按杯卖，一杯 500 日元。可以缝在手提包上，也可以制成胸针或首饰。可以买来尝试看看。

Full of handicrafts articles such as buttons, beads and bobbin thread. Buttons are often sold by a bundle in a cup and it's suggested to attach them to your bags or remake them into brooches or accessories.

便携的小型家具或器物十分受欢迎。这些商品还是叫古器物更贴切。这些古器物所属的年代多为明治以后。因为价格实惠，购买没有任何负担，所以非常适合古董入门者。

Small furniture and utsuwa are popular. They were made after the Meiji era and are referred to as second-hand articles rather than antiques. They are sold at affordable prices, so they are recommended for beginners to start with.

如果遇到稀奇的器物，不知道是否产自日本，或不清楚其用途，可以直接问店主。可与平时很难逛到的店铺的老板直接交流，也是逛东京跳蚤市场的一大乐趣。

When you find an article that you are uncertain whether it was made in Japan or how to use it, ask the shop owner. Communicating with a shop owner you wouldn't usually meet is the fun part of Tokyo Nominoichi.

大木箱子里放满了各式各样的小箱子。有铝制餐盒、隔断式印章盒、旧茶罐等，可以把它们直接用作装饰品，当然，也可用于收纳，装一些小物件。

Mid-size wooden box are full of smaller boxes. Small boxes are aluminum lunch boxes, seal cases with a divider and old tea cans. They would look attractive being displayed as they are, or you can use them as a container for small things.

旧剪刀或钳子被陈列于墙壁或架子上时，可以在室内营造出工业风。通过观察它们的形状和生锈程度找到你喜欢的商品吧。

Tools such as old scissors and pincers are the articles that give industrious taste with the interior when displayed on the wall or shelf. Find your favorite item by looking at the shapes and rust condition.

锁

日本最古老的锁头是1998年在大阪野野上的遗迹中发现的海老锁，是飞鸟时代的器物。在《古事记》《源氏物语》中也有关于锁的文章。锁的历史比想象中更加久远。日本古代的锁多为门栓形式，锁更多是用在商人或武家（武士系统的家族、人物）的仓库、金库中，较少用于普通人家。随着岁月流逝，锁的结构变得越来越复杂，甚至有的锁中还精心设置了机关。

LOCK AND KEY

The oldest key found in Japan was an “*Ebi-jyo*” excavated from Nonoue remains in Osaka in 1998, and is said to have been made in the Asuka era. Keys have a surprisingly long history as they were referred to in the “Kojiki” and “Genji monogatari.” Japanese old keys were made mostly with the crossbar and used at the storehouse or safe of the merchant or samurai but rarely used by ordinary people. Throughout the years the structure of keys became more complicated and mechanical by careful study.

招财猫

关于招财猫的起源，众说纷纭，其中，被人们普遍认可的是招财猫起源于浅草的今户烧或世田谷的豪德寺的说法。因为猫会驱赶老鼠，所以自古以来猫一直被视为象征生意兴旺的吉祥物。据说举起右手的招财猫可以招财运，举起左手的招财猫可以招贵人。一般的招财猫模型都是模仿三毛猫的形象，也有驱魔除邪的黑猫、消除病魔的红猫等版本。古代烧制的招财猫饶有趣味，精巧可爱。

MANEKINEKO

There are many theories on the origin of Manekineko. Among them, “Imado ware” in Asakusa and “Goutokuji” in Setagaya are leading. From long ago, people believed Manekineko to be a bringer of good luck for a thriving business. It is said that Manekineko raising the right paw invite economic fortune, and ones raising the left paw invite good people. Generally, they are modeled after calico cat. Other variations are the black cat for protecting from evil and misfortune and the red cat for protecting from illness. Manekineko of old times have a typically cute but retro-nuanced face.

⑩ 猿山古董店（麻布十番）

该店铺位于一所老公寓中，打开门，在眼前延伸开来的是一片白色的空间，可以感受到一种清冷的氛围。器物等距排列于米黄色的日本古家具上。店主猿山修先生不愧是设计师，陈列方式都是经过精心设计的，突出了每一个器物的特点。“店铺已经开了近25年，原本是作为产品资料的需要而开始收集古董，结果后来因堆积的古董太多，就开了这家店。古器物的魅力既在于反映了当时的时代特色，也在于器物本身。”现代的玻璃制品或小茶壶即使形状相同，成型方法也不同。有的是人工吹制成型，有的则是用“宙吹”法使之成型。即使设计相同，若使用的材质或制法不同，器物的感觉也会有区别。这恰是其有趣之处。经过猿山先生的甄选排列，在店里可以同时欣赏到古代和现代的设计。

(时) 13:00—18:00 (电) 03-3401-5935 (休)不定期 (址)港区元麻布 3-12-46 和光公寓 101 (交)地铁麻布十番站步行 5 分钟 (网)guillemets.net

⑩ SARUYAMA (Azabu-juban)

When stepping into a room of an old apartment where white is the main interior color, you are surrounded by a distinctive crisp feeling. Bowls and vases are lined up neatly in a right interval to the amber color old Japanese furniture, and the display is perfectly calculated to set off the shape of each item, thanks to the great designer, Osamu Saruyama, who runs the shop. "I have run this shop for almost 25 years. I started collecting antiques as a material for the products and the collection has grown so large to fully occupy the shop. I find old things interesting because they reflect the time they were made, and many are the only copies of their kind." Among contemporary glasses and tea pots that are in the same shape and displayed together, some are made by hand paring using a mold, and some are free blown. Even if the design is the same, the difference in the material and production method brings out a subtle variation. The design of old and modern works shows up through the filter of Saruyama.

(H) 13:00-18:00 (T) 03-3401-5935 (C) Irregular (Ad) 3-12-46 Motoazabu, Minato-ku, Wako mansion 101
(Ac) 5-min walk from Azabu-juban Station (Toei Line) (U) guillemets.net

古器物与现代作品展示在同一空间。洁白的墙面装点着复古灯具、钟表以及茶色的古家具。这里不定期举办现代艺术家的作品展，展品全部都经过了猿山先生的精心挑选。

Old articles and the products of contemporary artists are displayed together in the shop. The white wall makes the lightings and clocks assembled by old parts and brown old furniture more attractive. The exhibitions of contemporary artists are held randomly and artists must be selected by Saruyama's high standard.

⓫ 古董店 tamiser（惠比寿）

门上写着小小的店名 tamiser，推门走进去后，眼前呈现的是笼罩着柔和灯光的空间。店主吉田昌太郎从世界各地收集到的古器物井井有条地摆放在店内，整个空间满满当当的，整体十分和谐。吉田先生挑选器物的标准就是要吸引自己，无论是衣物、食物或是建造住宅的器物，都要具有相同的吸引力。吉田先生按照自己的感觉挑选出来的器物，既有国外博物馆展出的珍品，也有不到 1 000 日元就可以买到的古器具、古玩等。它们在吉田先生心中占据着同样的地位。宽大的桌子上摆放的白色器物，有的白中带青，有的略泛黄色，形状、厚度也各不相同，在其中进行甄选不失为一种乐趣。吉田先生说道："经常研究古代器物使我对这些器物和时间的感觉都发生了变化：距离我们较近的是昭和时代，想来也快有 100 年的历史了，但我却觉得更久远的江户时代离我更近，仿佛近在身边。"

(时)12:00—19:00 (电)03-6277-2085 (休)星期一 (址)涩谷区惠比寿 3-22-1 (交)JR 惠比寿站步行 8 分钟 (网)tamiser.com

⓫ Antiques tamiser (Ebisu)

Once you step in the shop, you are surrounded by the soft light filling it. Every antique collected by Shotaro Yoshida from all over the world gives you a somewhat tense impression but with an affectionate look. "Whether choosing clothes and food or building a house, you should choose them based on the same standard because they are drawn to each other by the same energy," said Yoshida. That's why things picked up by him based on his energy and sense include not only priceless pieces that can be exhibited at overseas museums but also second-hand articles and antiques less than ¥1,000 in value on the same stage. White dishes displayed on the big table are arranged according to the color such as blue, yellow and others that contain basic white. Each has its individuality in the shape and thickness. It's fun to find a favorite. "I feel like the Edo era is quite recent when I am handling old articles. Articles of Showa will be 100 years old after a couple of years. That thought may alter my feeling towards old things and time," he said.

Ⓗ12:00-19:00 Ⓣ03-6277-2085 Ⓒ Monday (Ad)3-22-1 Ebisu Shibuya-ku (Ac)8-min walk from JR Ebisu Station (JR Line) Ⓤtamiser.com

这里原本是一间洗车场，后来被改造成了店铺。加高的地面也是原本留下的痕迹。空间用门窗进行了隔断，一侧是吉田先生的私人空间，另一侧的书以及箱子的摆放方法都非常值得借鉴。

The former auto repair shop. The inside was remodeled into shop space. A floor slightly raised above the main shop floor still remains. The other side divided by the door and window is the office space of Yoshida. It is full of his style. You will want to steal his display sense of books and boxes.

EASE KEEP
HIS SPACE
OPEN

这里堆叠的几个木箱子，原本是用来盛放入窑烧制之前的瓷器的，现在摇身一变成了花瓶的舞台。箱子表面还留有木材的白色痕迹，展现了质朴的自然之美。古代的花瓶，即便不用来插花，只是作为装饰摆放在那里，也有一种天然的存在感。

A vase on the stage of wooden boxes piled up. The boxes were the containers for the vases before being baked in a kiln. The patterns on the surface of the box are remains of white soil showing the natural unmodified beauty. An antique vase shows its presence, even without a flower.

桃山时代的唐津烧（30000 日元）、明治时代的平佐烧（12000 日元）、江户时代后期的白丹波（80000 日元），这些器物的烧制时间、地区各不相同，现在却同时存在于同一空间、同一张桌子上。它们与任何一道菜品都能完美契合，形成独特的氛围。

Karatsu ware of the Momoyama era (¥30,000), Hirasa ware of Meiji era (¥12,000), Shirotannba of the late Edo era (¥80,000) and others, were produced in different times and places, but are now displayed on the same table. Every plate has an air of great luxury that would make any dish served on it look gorgeous.

笔墨盒

笔墨盒形状类似于烟管或长管，是笔筒与墨水盒合二为一的便携式文具盒。笔筒出现于镰仓时代，在此之上附带墨水盒则是从江户时代开始的。笔墨盒多为黄铜或紫铜制，为了方便携带而制作得非常结实。有的可以放入刀刃，有的可以放入两支笔，设计多种多样，还有的描绘了莳绘图案，展现了每个时代不同的流行设计。

YATATE

Yatate looks like a Japanese smoking pipe but it's a portable writing tool case in which a writing brush and ink are integrated. Production of yatate started from the Kamakura era and an inkpot was added from the Edo era. Characteristically, it was made of solid brass or copper for carrying. There were many design variations. One was designed to insert a small sword and another to have one holder for two writing brushes. Some designs were more elaborate such as using makie technique and popular designs changed with the times.

医疗用品

随着日本医疗技术的发展，医疗用品的制造技术也不断进步。由于可以从中窥见医疗的发展历史，因此受到收藏家的喜欢。药瓶、烧杯、烧瓶等玻璃制品经常被用作室内装饰物，由于数量多、价格优惠，很容易买到。在手工时代制作的一些产品，具有古代的玻璃独有的流动感和质感，颜色也并非完全透明，反而独具魅力。

MEDICAL DEVICES

Production technology of medical devices has advanced with the progress of medical techniques in Japan. Medical devices are popular items to learn the medical history in Japan. However, glass products such as medicine bottles, beakers and flasks are mostly demanded for interior items. You can easily obtain them because they were produced in large quantities and the prices are affordable. Products from the handmade days are preferred for their fluctuation, plumpness and slightly unclear color.

⑫ 灰狼杂货店与西别府花店（青山）

2011 年开业的杂货店“灰狼”，2014 年变为灰狼杂货店与西别府花店的结合体，以崭新的面貌重新开业。店铺的理念是“古老”与“生机”，“灰狼”负责古器物的采购，西别府花店负责植物、插花的采购。历经了悠久岁月的古器物和充满生命力的植物，两种原本完全相反的事物，被展示在同一家店内，时间仿佛停止了一般，营造出一个时光缓慢流逝的独特空间。古器物主要包含俄罗斯的器物，也有日本的器物。店主挑选商品时不论国籍，只选择民间手工艺品以及日常用品，所以一眼望去无法分清其国籍，甚是有趣。店内有许多令人惊叹的器物，每一件都会激起人的创作欲望。店铺发挥自身特色，创作出将古器物和植物融为一体的原创艺术品，在全国各地进行展出。

(时)11:00—20:00（星期日 19:00 闭店）(电)03-3478-5073 (休)全年无休（可能会临时休业）(址)港区南青山 3-15-2 公寓南青山 102 室 (交)地铁表参道站步行 8 分钟 (网)hairo-ookami.com

⓬ Haiiro Ookami + Hanaya Nishibeppu Shoten (Aoyama)

"Dogu to Zakka Haiiro Ookami"started in 2011 and it was remodeled to "Haiiro Ookami + Hanaya Nishibeppu Shoten" in 2014. Haiiro Ookami procures second-hand articles under the theme of "old" and Nishibeppu Shoten procures miscellaneous goods and fresh flowers under the theme of "alive". Second-hand articles sitting there after many years and plants full of vitality are displayed together in the same shop. The contrast between them in the same room creates a strange feeling as if time has frozen. Second-hand articles are collected from Russia and Japan but mainly from Russia. On the other hand, folk craft goods and everyday life goods are collected regardless of the origin of the country so, interestingly, nationality is hardly recognizable in them. Just watching all the strange things and parts are displayed and watching them all will surely excite your creativity. Original artwork of the shop mixing plants and second-hand articles is also displayed across the country as an exhibition.

Ⓗ11:00-20:00 (Sunday -19:00) Ⓣ03-3478-5073 Ⓒ No holiday (temporarily closed) (Ad)3-15-2 Minami Aoyama Minato-ku, Mansion Minami Aoyama 102 (Ac)8-min walk from Omote Sando Station (Toei Line) Ⓤ hairo-ookami.com

⑬ OTSU 家具店（目黑）

OTSU 家具店是一家日本古董家具店，坐落于目黑大街。这一整条街都是家装设计店铺，所以被称为家具街。该店的经营理念是：将精美的古器物传承到下一代。店内收集了自明治时代到昭和时代中期的日本古董家具。店内收藏的家具，有的体现了日本手工艺人精湛的技艺、精妙的设计，有的拥有美妙的木材纹理，每一件家具都制作精良，让人想一直传承使用下去。日式橱柜、灯具、桌子等，有的设计简约，有的独具匠心，种类丰富，并且设计丝毫不会有陈旧的感觉，可以完美地融入现代生活。每一件家具都保存完好，没有用过古家具的顾客可以尝试。店里有适合独居小房间的折叠矮脚餐桌和小书架，也有能够收纳大量餐具的餐具柜，还有适合宽敞房间的大桌子和高大的架子，无论房间大小如何，都能够找到尺寸合适的家具。

㊐11:00—20:00 ㊉03-3794-7883 ㊡全年无休（除元旦前后）㊗目黑区鹰番 1-4-9 ㊫东急东横线学艺大学站步行 10 分钟 ㊋demode-furniture.net/otsu

⓭ OTSU FURNITURE (Meguro)

Otsu Furniture, specializing in Japanese old furniture is located at Meguro-dori commonly known by "Kagu-Dori (furniture street)" with many interior shops. Plenty of old Japanese furniture from Meiji through the mid-Showa era is collected under the theme of "Hand down good old things for posterity." Only Japanese furniture with pretty grain patterns and firmly made by the design of highly-skilled Japanese masters is displayed to be used and also handed down for posterity. Wadansu, cupboards, lightings and desks are displayed by a number of variations from simple to elaborate designs. The designs are timeless and fit a modern life. Beautifully maintained furniture is recommended for the absolute beginners. Furniture of all sizes to fit any house can be found, for example, chabudai and a small book shelf for small room of someone living alone, a big cupboard with a capacity for the person with a lot of dishes and a large table and shelf for the owner of a large house.

(H) 11:00-20:00 (T) 03-3794-7883 (C) No holiday (except Year-end and New Year holidays) (Ad) 1-4-9 Takaban Meguro-ku (Ac) 10-min walk from Gakugei Daigaku Station (Tokyu Line) (U) demode-furniture.net/otsu

⑭ CASICA 集合店（新木场）

2017 年 11 月，一直被称为木材街区的新木场内，出现了一家引起热议的选物商店——CASICA。CASICA 的品牌理念是：将我们存在的时间和空间可视化，因此为店铺起名 CASICA（在日语中是可视化的意思）。设计者将家具、艺术、设计、手工艺人、工作室、美食、影像等全部概念汇集在同一个空间。因为店铺运营方是一家影像制作公司，所以这里不仅是店铺，也设立了摄影棚、录音室等。原本专注于表现眼前所见事物的专家们，现在开辟了一个全新的空间，来表现肉眼看不见的事物。在店铺巨大的空间内，有上下互通的画廊，有进行古家具修缮及制作的工作室，有主打药膳、颇具熟食店风格的咖啡厅。店铺内有古器物以及日本传统工艺制作的生活杂货，商品的甄选无关时代、价格、国家或民族，唯一标准就是器物本身的魅力。

㊐11:00—19:00 ㊀03-6457-0826（店铺 / 店主）、03-6457-0827（咖啡厅）㊡星期一 ㊟江东区新木场 1-4-6 ㊋JR 新木场站步行 3 分钟 ㊔casica.tokyo

⑭ CASICA (Shinkiba)

CASICA is a much talked-about shop that opened in Nov. 2017 at Shinkiba, commonly known as "wood town". The shop was named CASICA after the concept of "Visualization (Casica) of ever-changing time and space". Everything from furniture and products, art and design, craftsmen and studios, and food and film were brought together in one place. CASICA is based on a video production company therefore not only shops, but also photo studios and recording rooms are combined. Professionals in expressing visible things have created this place to visualize invisible things. The huge building space holds a gallery with an open ceiling 13m high, an atelier to produce and repair the furniture, a delicatessen-style café serving mainly medicinal dishes and a studio. Not only second-hand articles and old wares, but also household goods manufactured by Japanese traditional techniques and goods selected for their attractiveness regardless of price, time, country and ethnicity are sold in the shop.

Ⓗ11:00-19:00 Ⓣ03-6457-0826 (shop/main) 03-6457-0827 (café) Ⓒ Monday (Ad) 1-4-6 Shinkiba Koto-ku (Ac) 3-min walk from Shinkiba Station (JR Line) Ⓤ casica.tokyo

印刷品

古代印刷品的设计十分有趣，并且还可以从中得知当时的潮流和风俗习惯。海报、传单、火柴盒以及玩具的盒子等，使用了许多现代没有的非常柔和的颜色，一些双色或黑白印刷的物品也十分有趣。点心的包装纸以及千代纸（一种有彩色图纹的日本纸）等具有昭和时代复古风情的设计，让人不禁怀念起童年时光。

PRINTED MATTER

It is a real pleasure that we can learn not only the interesting designs but also the trends, manners and customs of the times from old printed matter. Posters, leaflets, matchbox labels and toy packages were printed with soft colors that are currently not available, and it's interesting to see two-color printing or items colored after printing in monochrome. Sweets wrapping paper and *Chiyogami* (Japanese paper with colored figures) printed with a retro styled design of the early Showa era bring us back to the childhood.

赛璐珞

赛璐珞是 1856 年在英国发明出来的、史上最早的一批人工合成树脂，在日本也极受欢迎。其最初是作为象牙的替代品开发出来的，用硝酸纤维素及樟脑等合成。许多人可能都用过多彩的大理石纹样的笔盒。因为这一材质容易加热成型，所以也会被用来加工成盒子、钢笔、眼镜、人偶等。进入 21 世纪，人们开发出了新的塑料材质，现在已经基本不再使用赛璐珞。

CELLULOID

Celluloid is the first synthetic resin in history and was invented in England as a substitute for ivory that was popular also in Japan in 1856 and made of nitrocellulose, camphor and others. Many people may have owned celluloid pencil cases imitating tortoiseshell or with a pattern of colorful marbles. Fountain pens, glasses and dolls have been made of celluloid because it's easy to mold by heat. Celluloid has been replaced by new plastic invented in 20th century and is hardly produced anymore.

第三章

装点餐桌的器物

OLD THINGS FOR KITCHEN AND DINING

与古器物的相遇是一生一次的邂逅，尽情体会探寻的乐趣与使用的喜悦

受到喜爱古器物的祖母的影响，沟口女士从小就开始使用古器物。“对我而言，古器物就是我从小使用的日常用品。器物只有被使用才会有生命力。后来我开始在茶寮中使用古器物，就是希望可以让更多人体会到这一点。”沟口女士使用的古器物多是自己从古董集市精心挑选的，或是购自信任的古董店、丈夫开的“白日”古董店（见第 88 页）。“古器物的魅力在于它的个性，它的独一无二。”沟口女士说，“与古器物的相遇是‘一期一会’。因此，善于发现的眼睛和决断力显得十分重要。首先要大胆地推门进来。对于认真观看的顾客，我一定会热情接待的。”

Finding an old piece of utsuwa is a once-in-lifetime experience Enjoy the process of searching it and have fun using it

Mizoguchi has used old utsuwa since childhood influenced by her grandmother. “For me it’s a familiar thing. The more you use the utsuwa, the more you understand the value of it. That’s why I also use old pieces in saryo for everyone to realize that.” She buys old utsuwa mostly at her husband’s shop Hakujitsu (p88), antique markets or reliable antique shops. She says, “Old utsuwa that I own reflect my personality and they are one of a kind. You need trained eyes and decisiveness to find an old one of a kind piece. Now just open the door. Every earnest guest will be treated kindly.”

ARTRIP ADVISER
艺术之旅顾问

沟口实穗
Miho Mizoguchi

位于东京浅草鸟越的预约制实体茶寮店铺“九个点心屋”（开授和果子制作课程）店主。沟口女士自己学习了日本的传统文化，然后通过自己的方式传授给别人，并以此作为职业。茶寮中使用的器物以及店主挑选器物的品位都受到顾客好评。

Miho Mizoguchi runs “Kashiya Kokonotsu Saryo” (serving Japanese sweet course, reservation required) at Asakusa Torigoe, Tokyo. Her business is to offer lessons to learn Japanese traditions through experience and hand it down in one’s own way. Selection sense of utsuwa and tools used at her saryo have a good reputation.

古董集市

⑮ 富冈八幡宫古董集市、青空集市（门前仲町）

富冈八幡宫于 1927 年建成，是江户最大的八幡神像所在地。神社内有一尊日本“地图之祖”——测量家伊能忠敬的铜像。据说他每次出发去日本各地测量之前，必定先来这里参拜。这里每月第 1 和第 2 个星期日会举办古董集市，共有一百多家书店、玩具店、古伊万里瓷器店参展，第 1 个星期日展出的主要是西方古董，第 2 个星期日则主要是东方古董。在这里，人们可以在大量的杂货中挖掘宝贝，也可以品评摆放有序的美术品，可以与店主交流喜欢的古董，也可以享受自由的氛围。每月 15 日和 28 日会举办青空集市，售卖手工艺品和日常用品。每到这时，神社内就熙熙攘攘，挤满了探寻珍品的人们。参加青空集市时，还可以顺便去附近永代大道的商业街和在参道举办的深川庙会（每月 1 日、15 日、28 日）逛一逛。也有许多外国游客来这里，一边拿着章鱼烧或今川烧大快朵颐，一边漫步于古董集市或商业街中。

(时) 古董集市是每月第 1、第 2 个星期日，青空集市是每月 15 日和 28 日。从日出开放到日落
(电) 03-3451-0537 (费) 免费 (址) 江东区富冈 1-20 (交) 地铁门前仲町站步行 6 分钟 (网) www.kotto-rakuichi.com tomioka-aozora.jp

⑮ Tomioka Hachimangu Antique Market / Flea Market (Monzennakacho)

In the precinct of *Tomioka Hachimangu*, there is a bronze statue of Ino Tadataka, a geographical surveyor who drew the first-ever detailed map of Japan. He was said to have visited that place before leaving for a geographical survey trip. An antique market is held on every first and second Sunday with over 100 stalls of books, toys and Ko-Imari. The first Sunday is for Western antiques and the second Sunday mainly for Oriental antiques. You can enjoy Shitamachi home-like market when hunting treasures or assessing art works or talking with a shop owner about your favorite antiques. On every 15th and 28th, an open market is held for antiques and for handcrafted articles and daily necessaries. The precinct gets crowded with people picking up bargains. Let's visit Fukagawa Ennichi (a fair on every 1st, 15th and 28th) held at an entrance path and shopping street along the Eitai-Dori nearby. Foreigners can also enjoy strolling through the Ennichi, eating takoyaki and obanyaki.

Ⓗ Antique Market: 1st, 2nd Sunday every month Flea Market: 15th and 28th every month both from sunrise to sunset Ⓣ 03-3451-0537 Ⓕ Free (Ad) 1-20 Takaoka Koto-ku (Ac) 6-min walk from Monzen-nakacho Station (Toei Line) Ⓤ www.kotto-rakuichi.com tomioka-aozora.jp

⑯ 鲁山器物店（西荻洼）

在被称为古董古玩街的西荻洼，“鲁山”是一个十分重要的存在。“鲁山”由大岛文彦先生创立于 1982 年，他本人把店铺称为餐具店。店内摆放的器物有玻璃、陶瓷，材质多样，大小不一，古代器物与现代器物相互融合。乍一看上去，很难分辨哪一个是古代的，哪一个是现代的。这得益于大岛先生挑选器物的慧眼。他说：“餐具是用来享受生活的，是用来使用的，会使生活丰富多彩。不要把古器物看作古董，当作生活用品就好了。”该店铺的一大魅力就在于大岛先生的人品和谈吐。店内似乎有一种吸引人的力量，即使是初次造访的人，也会不自觉地坐在沙发上，一边喝茶一边放松下来，像是这里的常客。这里每个月都会举办陶艺艺术家的展览，展览信息可以通过网站获取。不妨怀着探寻餐具、丰富生活的想法来这里看一看。

㊐ 11:00—19:00 ㊉ 03-3399-5036 ㊡ 星期二 ㊟ 杉并区西荻北 3-45-8 西荻 PER-SONARE 大楼 1 层 ㊋ JR 西荻洼站步行 8 分钟 ㊒ ro-zan.com

⑯ ROZAN (Nishiogikubo)

"Rozan" is a very important shop in Nishi-Ogikubo, an antiques town. "Rozan" was opened 35 years ago by Fumihiko Oshima, a potter, and he calls this shop "Shokkiya" (tableware shop). The shop displays tableware made of glass or ceramics in various sizes and by old or contemporary craftsmen all together. Tableware of old and modern fit into the shop atmosphere and can hardly be distinguished at a glance. It must be attributed to the intuition of Oshima. He says, "Tableware has to be used as a tool to enjoy life and to fill it with happiness and blessing. Let's look at the old utsuwa as a tool in your life, not as an antique." His nice personality, his knowledge and stories are so attractive in the shop that even first-time visitors will find themselves sitting on the sofa with a cup of tea at hand just like a long time regular customer. An exhibition is held for the products by potters every month. Check the schedule on the web before visiting. You will find tableware that will enrich your life.

(H) 11:00-19:00 (T) 03-3399-5036 (C) Tuesday (Ad) 3-45-8 Nishiogi Kita Suginami-ku, PER-SONARE Nishiogi 1st floor (Ac) 8-min walk from Nishiogikubo Station (JR Line) (U) ro-zan.com

大岛先生还会用铁来制作器物。照片中的灯罩就出自大岛先生之手。店内随意摆放着许多用作材料的铁或木头。大岛先生故意将阿拉丁煤油炉的涂料剥除，这样反而使火炉更具韵味。

Oshima surprisingly uses iron for his products. All the lampshades displayed here are made by him. Materials such as iron, wood and others are located in an offhand way in the shop. The well-used looking stove was made by deliberately peeling off the blue paint of the frame of the Aladdin stove.

剑尖杯

剑尖杯的出现年代是大正至昭和时代初期，因为杯上的图案与剑尖相似，故得名“剑尖杯”。这一设计来源于欧洲，但是日本的剑尖杯更重，另一大特点是有气泡。剑尖杯虽然看起来小巧精致，但实际拿在手中就能感受到它的重量，这是因为剑尖杯是用高纯度的铅玻璃制作而成。剑尖杯是在古董集市中都难得一见的珍品。

KENZAKI GLASS

The *Kenzaki* glass made between the Taisho era and the beginning of the Showa era gained its name from the pattern of spear blades pointed upwards that it bears all around the glass. Its design originated in Europe, but the Japanese version is unique in that it is made of thicker glass and contains air bubbles. Although the glass is small, it is heavy because it is made of high-grade lead glass. Kenzaki glass is very rare even in antique markets.

荞麦盅

荞麦盅是用来盛放荞麦面蘸汁的小杯子。原本还用来盛放向付（日本会席料理中的一道菜，是季节性的生鱼片），用途广泛。江户时代荞麦面开始流行，这种形状的器皿就被叫作荞麦盅了。日本的古器物多采用青花或赤绘手法制成，荞麦盅是伊万里瓷器的一种，从手绘到触感柔软的蒟蒻印判，再到平价的印判，荞麦盅中采用的彩绘手法多种多样。

SOBA CHOKO

This *Ochoko* (sake cup), also known as *Soba Choko*, is used as a dipping cup for soba noodles. It was originally used for various purposes such as to serve Mukozukē, but since soba noodles became popular during the Edo era, these cups became to be called Soba Choko. Most traditional Japanese soba choko are either sometsuke or akae style. The soba choko of Imari are made through various techniques from hand painting to stamping the design which produces a softer color, or reasonably priced transferware technique.

⑰古董店 poubelle（西荻洼）

2014 年，古董古玩街西荻洼新开了一家店——“poubelle”，店铺的经营理念是“店内有神物”。店内陈列着店主矢泽刚先生挑选的古董以及他本人的作品。矢泽刚先生每年 11 月都会举办个展，在国外也十分活跃，2017 年还在上海举办过活动。矢泽先生介绍，开店的契机是想自己做点事情。矢泽先生从高中起就喜欢古器物，享受以优惠的价格入手稀缺物品的乐趣。古董也是同样，寻找价格亲民且品质上乘的器物，恰能体现挑选的技术。矢泽先生说：“我进行挑选的时候，不一定都是挑选古器物。不论古老的或现代的，我只选择自己喜欢的，包括颜色、形状、质感。”店内摆放的器物、刀具、古陶瓷、装饰品等，都给人一种静谧的感觉。这大概就是矢泽先生所喜爱的空灵感吧。这家店铺让人不禁想要多次访问，去感受矢泽先生的世界观及其挑选古董的品位。

㊉11:00—19:30 ㊊090-1540-7133 ㊡星期二 ㊟杉并区西荻北 3-42-5 ㊇JR 西荻洼站步行 5 分钟 ㊋poubelle0702.jimdo.com

⑰ poubelle (Nishiogikubo)

In 2014, a new shop opened in Nishi-Ogikubo, a town of antiques, and the shop's concept is "a shop full of obsessions." The shop displays antiques that have been selected or created by shop manager Yazawa and restored pieces of work. He holds an annual exhibition in November, actively promotes antiques abroad, and had an exhibition in Shanghai in 2017. It seems that he "wanted to try something on his own." Yazawa liked old items since he was in high school. He seemed to enjoy looking for hidden gems. Antiques are similar in this way, as finding quality pieces for a reasonable price is the test of one's skill. "It doesn't necessarily have to be old. I collect pieces that I like in terms of color, shape, and quality, regardless of whether they are old or new." The tableware, cutlery, antique china, objets d'art, and all other pieces in the shop seem to create tranquility. Perhaps this is what Yazawa likes to feel. It is a shop that entices many visitors to feel and taste its view of the world.

(H) 11:00-19:30 (T) 090-1540-7133 (C) Tuesday (Ad) 3-42-5 Nishiogikita, Suginami-ku (Ac) 5-min walk from Nishi-Ogikubo Station (JR Line) (U) poubelle0702.jimdo.com

隐僻的古董店白日（浅草桥）

A HIDDEN GALLERY AND SHOP OF SECOND-HAND ARTICLES HAKUJITU (Nishiogikubo)

古董店“白日”原本位于台东区鸟越，2018 年春天迁到柳桥。现在的店铺原本是一家牙科诊所，是拥有 100 年历史的建筑。店铺的理念是将被埋没的物品展示在聚光灯下。原本埋没在各个角落的古器物，被店主西坂晃一先生发掘，展现在了充满柔和光线的空间里。西坂先生甄选器物的原则就是适合装饰。今后店铺也会与现代艺术家及制造商合作，创造出“一个人生命中不可缺少的物品”。让我们拭目以待。

A shop of second-hand articles called *Hakujitu*, which was in Torigoe, Taito-ku, relocated and reopened in spring of 2018. The new location is a 100-year-old former dental clinic building. Hakujitu's concept is to shed light on pieces that have been hidden, and the shop will undoubtedly shine the world's light upon antique pieces safely recovered by the owner Koichi Nishizaka after being forgotten somewhere in Japan. It is exciting to think of one-of-a-kind pieces for new display, and his project with modern writers and manufacturers to create “things needed in a person's life.”

白日（浅草桥）

(时) 营业时间不定，需要提前咨询 (电) 090-8568-5355 (址) 台东区柳桥 1-24-4
(网) www.instagram.com/hakujitu_

HAKUJITU (Asakusabashi)

(H) tbc, please call to confirm (T) 090-8568-5355 (Ad) 1-24-4 Yanagibashi, Taito-ku
(U) www.instagram.com/hakujitu_

这一片展区的主题是“眺望远山”。西坂先生介绍：“古器物之所以历经岁月洗礼，仍然没有被遗弃，留传至今，是有它的理由的，这就是古器物的魅力。”

“My displays create the feeling of looking at a distant mountain.” “The beauty of old pieces is their uniqueness that made them survive till now without being abandoned,” says Nishizaka.

从东京可以当天往返，
前往古器物爱好者的“圣地”——益子的仁平古家具店

仁平古家具店益子店（益子）

从东京到栃木县益子町，驱车需两个小时，乘坐电车及公交需两个半小时。益子地区从江户时代开始就以陶瓷而闻名，如今因每年 4 月和 11 月会举办益子陶器集市而被人们熟知。集市主要展示当地艺术家创造的器物及工艺品。仁平古家具店益子店，是古器物爱好者必会造访的店铺。店铺附近还有两家姊妹店。可以当成一场短途旅行去逛一逛。

㊐11:00—18:00 ㊝0285-70-6007 ㊡星期四 ㊤栃木县芳贺郡益子町益子 3435 ㊥真冈铁路真冈线益子站步行 25 分钟 ㊦www.nihei-furukagu.com

One-Day Trip from Tokyo
to Mashiko

NIHEI-FURUKAGU MASHIKO BRANCH (Mashiko)

This shop is located in the town of Mashiko, Tochigi prefecture, which is a 2-hour car ride or a 2.5-hour train and bus ride from Tokyo. Since the Edo era, Mashiko has flourished as a pottery town, and is famous for the Mashiko Pottery Market in April and November, in which tableware and crafts created by local artists are displayed. In Mashiko, Nihei-Furukagu is the place to go for antique-lovers. There are 2 other shops in the vicinity of Mashiko, which would be nice to visit on a small trip.

(H) 11:00-18:00 (T) 0285-70-6007 (C) Thursday (Ad) 3435 Mashiko, Mashikomachi, Haga-gun, Tochigi pref. (Ac) 25-min walk from Mashiko Station (Mouka Railway) (U) www.nihei-furukagu.com

店内正在使用的古家具也可以购买。店内的货架较浅，摆放着的小盘子200日元起，价格十分实惠。即便是相同的盘子，每一个都呈现出不同的样态，这也是店内古器物的独特之处。歪斜的印花、不同的颜色，都赋予了它们独特韵味。

All of the old furniture used to display the tableware is also for sale. Among the displayed utsuwa, the small plates start at a reasonable price of ¥200. Every old piece of utsuwa is unique despite the same shape. The distortion in the design and differences in color are all part of the feature.

凳子3800日元起，长椅9800日元起，小桌子12800日元起，架子4800日元起，这在东京几乎是难以想象的低价。建议大家先量好需要的架子或抽屉的尺寸，再去店里采购。

Stools start from ¥3,800, benches from ¥9,800, small tables from ¥12,800, shelf units from ¥4,800. They are unbelievably low prices in Tokyo. It is recommended to first measure the space in your house to put the shelf units or chest of drawers before going to the shop.

室内装饰中的焦点是灯具。店内选用的都是玻璃灯罩，大多是自然风格、北欧风格，设计简单，又能很好地适应各种装饰风格。造型简单大方，多个叠加使用效果也很好。

The lights, as an important part of the interior, are fitted with glass shades. All designs are simple and are suitable for any interior including natural, Scandinavian, or any other style. Since they are not overpowering, multiple pieces can be used together in one room.

带有扶手的椅子也可以花10000日元左右买到手。凳子、长椅等，比餐具柜、书架等数量要少，所以如果能遇到喜欢的，真是非常幸运。店铺提供全国配送服务，所以即便冲动消费也无须顾虑。

This chair, with very sturdy arms, can be found for about ¥10,000. Stools, benches, and seats including armed chairs are rarely seen compared to china cabinets and bookshelves, so it would be true luck to find a chair you like. The store delivers nationwide making impulse purchases a viable option.

古建筑材料也极其丰富的仁平古家具店 1 号店

Antique Construction Articles, Nihei-Furukagu Shop No. 1

仁平古家具店真冈店（真冈）

店主仁平先生出生在真冈的邻镇，9 年前开了 1 号店。店铺附近就是工作室，共有 4 名工匠进行着修复工作。因为家具都是公司自己修复、销售，所以商品的价格十分亲民。

(时) 13:00—18:00 (电) 0285-81-5208 (休) 星期四 (址) 栃木县真冈市荒町 1095 (交) 真冈铁路真冈线益子站步行 15 分钟 (网) www.nihei-furukagu.com

NIHEI-FURUKAGU MOUKA BRANCH (Mouka)

This shop is the first branch started 9 years ago by the owner Nihei, who was born and raised in the town next to Mouka. He owns a workshop nearby where he has 4 craftsmen doing the maintenance work. Since his company also does restorations, everything is sold at reasonable prices.

(H) 13:00-18:00 (T) 0285-81-5208 (C) Thursday (Ad) 1095 Aramachi, Mouka-shi, Tochigi pref. (Ac) 15-min walk from Mouka Station (Mouka Railway) (U) www.nihei-furukagu.com

这里原本是一家糖果店店主的家，后来被改造成了现在的古家具店。家具全部提供全国配送服务，所以大可放心坐电车来买。2 层展示的是原创定制家具。

The shop has been renovated using the living quarters of a family-owned candy shop. All furniture can be delivered domestically, so you can visit by train. Custom made furniture is displayed on the 2nd floor.

这里有许多嵌有古玻璃的门、拉门等，在房屋改造时可以用到，也可以用作柜子门或隔断，受到众多进行室内翻新的人、DIY（自己动手制作）爱好者的欢迎。

Many fittings such as door and sliding door with antique glass panels are also available. This shop is popular with home renovators and DIY fans searching for room dividers or doors for shelf units.

大件的古家具，与店内的古器物相得益彰

A special place with large furniture, perfect for the shop interior

器物商店 Pejite（益子）

Pejite 位于益子的旧商业街中一条僻静的小路上。建筑本身已经有 60 年历史，由大谷石（在日本宇都宫市大谷町附近开采的石材）建造的米仓改造而来，空间宽阔。店内摆放着质量上乘的日本古家具、益子当地手工艺人制作的器物等各类日常生活用品和服饰。

㊍11:00—18:00 ㊓ 0285-81-5494 ㊡ 星期四 ㊢ 栃木县芳贺郡益子町益子 973-6
㊈ 真冈铁路真冈线益子站步行 7 分钟 ㊫ www.pejite-mashiko.com

pejite (Mashiko)

The shop is located on a quiet street in Mashiko. It is a renovated and spacious 60-year-old former rice storehouse constructed from *Oyaishi*. The shop displays Japanese old furniture, as well as utsuwa and clothes made by local artists.

(H)11:00-18:00 (T)0285-81-5494 (C)Thursday (Ad)973-6 Mashiko, Mashikomachi, Haga-gun, Tochigi pref. (Ac)7-min walk from Mashiko Station (Moka Railway)
(U)www.pejite-mashiko.com

店铺直接沿用了米仓的外观，风格别致。向当地工匠定做的木门也营造出一种独特的氛围。店铺门前还有开阔的空间可供停车。

The shop has a stylish exterior incorporating the essence of the storehouse. The wooden entrance door, ordered from a local artist, has a beautiful presence. There is an ample parking space.

印判

印判是一种日本陶瓷彩绘技法。与手绘不同，印判是像蜡纸一样通过复写将图案印在陶瓷上的方式，所以同一种图案的陶瓷可以进行量产。另外，由于印判使用的是一种叫作“柏林蓝”的化学染料，所以呈现出了与以往不同的蓝色。用印判技法制成的瓷器给人的印象大多是老百姓使用的平价物品，但是由于复写是一门手工艺，一些印有珍稀图案、成色好的器物价格也十分昂贵。小盘子的价格在 1000 日元左右。

INBAN

This is one of the techniques of designing porcelain china. Unlike hand painting, inban (transferware) is made by transfering the design like stencil printing, which enables mass productions of pottery with the same design. Using Berlin blue chemical dye also helped to produce a different hue of blue. In the old days, stamping was seen as a cheap method used by the common people, but since it is also performed by hand, pottery with rare design, or pottery in good condition could sometimes become valuable. Small plates are available from about ¥1,000.

漆器

漆器是在木材上反复涂漆制成的传统工艺品。由于制作工艺繁杂、制作过程费力费神，所以漆器属于高级工艺品，但是在古董集市或古器物店，也可以找到平价的漆器。漆器历史悠久，一般认为漆器起源于日本。此前在北海道出土了约 9000 年前绳文时代前期的漆器。用于制作漆器的漆树是日本固有的树木种类。漆器的装饰手法包括在表面装饰金银的莳绘手法，以及镶嵌贝壳的螺钿手法等。

SHIKKI

Traditional craftwork made by brushing lacquer onto tableware. They are expensive because of the long production process and they require a lot of care, but can be found for a reasonable price at antique markets and second-hand articles shops. They have a long history, and since Shikki from 9,000 years ago (in the first half of the *Jomon* era) have been excavated in Hokkaido and the type of lacquer tree used to make them are indigenous to Japan, Shikki are also said to have originated in Japan. Decorating techniques include makie, and *raden*.

第四章

富有韵味的古布

OLD FABRICS

一边感受古布中蕴含的历史，一边享受天然材质的质感和色彩

古布（BORO）指的是日本海沿岸的东北地区及北陆地区的小村庄中使用的衣服或布。当时人们生活贫困，衣服破了用碎布修补，就可以继续使用很长时间。“看到这些，就会有一种和 100 年前的人们共享时间的感觉，仿佛穿越了时空一样。”和服、碎布等，留传下来的古布的形态多种多样。古布可以作为艺术品装饰在墙上，也可以用来制作其他物品。“使用天然材料制作的古布，即使洗濯多次，其韵味也是只增不减。用古布制作的和服，其上的色彩和花纹是那个时代特有的，更是百看不厌。”

Feel the essence of the past woven into old fabrics while enjoying the unique texture and color of natural material

BORO is the name of garments and fabrics that were worn in secluded villages in the Tohoku and Hokuriku areas along the coast of the Sea of Japan. Since the villagers were poor, they repaired their garments through patchwork and used them carefully for a long time. Fukayama said, “Looking at BORO garments gives me the feeling of going back in time to be with people who lived 100 years ago.” There are various types of old fabric besides BORO, such as Kimonos and Hagire. They are also popular as art pieces to hang on walls and are used as material to create new items. She also said, “The beauty of natural fabric is that they gain more texture after numerous washes. The colors and designs used in Kimonos often do not exist in modern times, and therefore never stop being captivating.”

ARTRIP ADVISER
艺术之旅顾问

深山由美子
Yumiko Fukayama

古布收藏家、经销商，出生于日本秋田县，在母亲的农村老家接触到古老的田间工作服后开始对古布产生兴趣。后来创立了自己的品牌“BORO note”，使用古布制作衣服和小物件，并时常举办展览。

Old fabric collector & dealer. Born in Akita prefecture, she gained interest in BORO after seeing old overalls at her mother' s family farm. She created the brand “BORO note,” which makes clothes and small items using BORO, and displays her work in exhibitions.

⑱ 町田天满宫古董集市（町田）

町田天满宫古董集市于每月 1 日在町田天满宫内举办。集市从日出一直开到日落，有的常客天不亮就已经到达这里，还有海外游客来参加。到中午，集市上人来人往，热闹非凡。集市内布局紧凑，逛起来十分方便，有来自日本各地的 130 多家店铺参展，因此非常有看点。该集市因参展的古布店铺众多而出名，尤其是古和服的展出量位列关东地区第一。有许多喜爱古和服的女性前来参加，通常参展的和服店的顾客络绎不绝。据爱知县一位每个月都来参展的店主介绍，许多店铺每次都会来参展，每次的展位基本固定。在这里可以快速找到感兴趣的店铺，还可以与经常参展的店主成为朋友。有时不经意间告知店主自己正在寻找的商品，店主下次就会带来。古董集市真是来多少次都不会厌倦。

㊐每月 1 日举办（11 月、1 月有变动），开放时间为 7:00—16:00 ㊁090-3314-1994 ㊂免费
㊃町田市原町田 1-21-5 ㊄JR 町田站步行 8 分钟 ㊅kanagawa-antique-market.crayonsite.net

⑱ Machida Tenmangu Garakuta Antique Market (Machida)

"Machida Tenmangu garakuta antique market" is held at the Machida Tenmangu temple on the first day of every month. This popular antique market is open from dawn until dusk and becomes a bustling market by noon with foreign tourists and groups of female shoppers. It is compact, easy to navigate, and more than 130 businesses come from all over Japan to sell their products, making it worth seeing. It is known for its large number of stalls of old fabric businesses, and boasts the highest number of exhibits of vintage Kimonos in the Kanto area, so it attracts many female customers who love retro Kimonos, and the Kimono stalls are always popular. According to a business owner from Aichi pref. who has a stall every month, most of the businesses have been coming here for many years and have a designated spot for their stalls. In other words, it is easy to find specific stalls and become familiar with owners by visiting a few times. Some businesses sometimes even bring products on-demand to the following market. It is worth visiting many times.

(H) First day of every month (dates change in November and January), 7:00-16:00 (T) 090-3314-1994
(F) Free (Ad) 1-21-5 Haramachida, Machida-shi (Ac) 8-min walk from Machida Station (JR Line)
(U) kanagawa-antique-market.crayonsite.net

集市于每月 1 日开市，即便是工作日也是熙熙攘攘，很有人气。如果想来挖掘珍宝，最好选择上午。这里的古董价格低廉，许多商品一枚硬币(100 或 500 日元) 就能买到，可以卸下高价的负担轻松购买。

This popular market held on the first day of every month becomes flooded with people even at noon on weekdays. It is therefore recommended to go in the morning for a good bargain. Many of the items can be purchased for ¥500, which makes this market a satisfying leisurely visit.

灯具

19 世纪 80 年代，电灯开始在日本普及。白炽灯发明于明治时代的 1879 年。虽然电灯历史短暂，但的确给日本人的生活带来了翻天覆地的变化。电灯发明之初是灯泡的形式，后来出现了灯罩等别致的设计。到大正时代，乳白色玻璃吊灯曾风靡一时。乳白色玻璃吊灯体现了浓浓的大正时代风情，是极受欢迎的装饰用品。

LIGHTS

Lights became widely used in Japan during the 1880s. It seems that incandescent lamps were invented in 1879, which is during the Meiji era. Although lights bear a brief history, they dramatically changed day-to-day life in Japan. Starting with a light bulb, lights became more creative in design with such additions as lampshades, and during the Taisho era, pendant lights made of milk glass started dominating the world. They are enduringly popular as representations of "Taisho era romanticism."

日本玻璃

日本真正开始制作玻璃是进入江户时代之后。外国商船将玻璃传入长崎，用于制作门窗等。在传统日式房屋中经常看到的花纹玻璃，蕴含了日本独有的技艺。据说这种玻璃是在没有窗帘的时代为了保护个人隐私而制作的。日本玻璃形式多样，比如精巧可爱的花纹玻璃、时尚摩登的条纹玻璃等，种类丰富。

JAPANESE GLASS

Glass became manufactured in Japan during the Edo era. It spread to Japan through western ships that arrived in Nagasaki, and became commonly used for tableware, windows, and doors. Decorated glass panels, which are often found in old Japanese houses, are full of creativeness that is distinct to Japan. It seems that these panels were made to maintain privacy in a time before curtains. There are plenty of variations ranging from glass panels with pretty decoration to modern wavy glass.

⑲ 古董店 ALL tomorrow's parties（町田）

店主富冈荣二先生原本从事废物回收工作，15 年前开了这家店铺。富冈先生此前参与过餐饮店的室内设计工作，在布置店铺时，他发挥特长，摆满了大型展板等大件器物，这是与其他古董店的不同之处。上下两层的店铺中，家具、杂货等物品风格多样，既有日式的，又有西式的。还有一处仓库，摆满了家具、灯具。店铺里还经常可以见到设计师及同行的其他店主，他们都十分期待能够发现新宝物。在本店，一万日元以下就可以买到古家具，这是得益于町田的地理位置。平价古家具也有专门的师傅进行维护保养，可以放心购买。还有宽大的毯子、小毛毯等，都可以成为家装设计的亮点，受到顾客的欢迎。有的商品没有摆放在店铺内，如果有想要的商品，可以直接询问。光临本店时还可以顺便去附近的町田天满宫的古董集市逛一逛。

㊐13:00—20:00 ㊓042-865-1380 ㊡星期一、星期二 (址)町田市金森东 1-3-19 (交)JR 町田站步行 10 分钟 (网)www.atptic.com

第四章

⑲ ALL tomorrow's parties (Machida)

This shop was started 15 years ago by the owner, Tomioka, who had previously owned a recycling business. This unique shop handles interior design for restaurants and other businesses, and therefore has a wide range of signboards and large fixtures uncommon at regular antique furniture shops and shops of second-hand articles. The two-storey shop sells Japanese-western fusion furniture and general merchandise, and the warehouse behind it is packed with miscellaneous furniture and lighting from ceiling to floor. It is known to attract designers and businesses excited by the prospect of finding something special. Old furniture can be found for ¥10,000 or less due to its location in Machida. Every furniture piece is properly maintained by specialists at the shop. The main old fabric products are multi-purpose blankets made of BORO and rugs. If you are looking for a particular item, please ask. It would make a good trip to visit this shop and the Machida Tenmangu Garakuta Antique Market.

(H) 13:00-20:00 (T) 042-865-1380 (C) Monday and Tuesday (Ad) 1-3-19 Kanamorihigashi, Machida-shi (Ac) 10-min walk from Machida Station (JR Line) (U) www.atptic.com

从地板到天花板，店铺内摆满商品，不断给人带来惊喜。商品风格多样、年代各不相同，走在店内仿佛置身迷宫一般。如果中意的商品摆放的位置太高，可以请店员帮忙取下。

It is an exciting space filled with second-hand articles from ceiling to floor. It is recommended to walk around this maze of Japanese-western fusion furniture and pieces from various decades to find a nice item. Ask the staff for assistance if items are difficult to reach.

⑳ 传统工艺品店森田（青山）

青山古董街从青山大道的南青山五丁目开始，直通到六本木大道。第二次世界大战后，道路两边聚集了多家古董店，因而这块区域有了这样的别称。现在，街道上写字楼、精品店逐渐增多，昔日的老古董店如今变成摩天大楼，传统工艺品店“森田”是保留下来的为数不多的古董店之一。店铺于 1965 年开业，历史悠久，成立之初主要经营民间工艺品，现在主要售卖古董、染织品。店中的商品除了江户时代至“二战”前的日本古布之外，还有日本染色技术的来源地——一些东南亚国家、中国、土耳其等的手工染织品。每一件商品都是在当地收集到的佳品，即便不是收藏家，也会一眼就爱上。被子、和服等古布制品，可以进行再加工，用来装裱边框成为装饰品，也可以用来制作桌布。“古布的魅力在于它柔软的质感，因为经过经年累月的使用。请一定来店里实际看看，感受一下。”

(时)10:00—19:00 (电)03-3407-4466 (休)全年无休 (址)港区南青山 5-12-2 仓泽大楼 1 层 (交)地铁表参道站步行 6 分钟 (网)morita-antiques.com

⑳ Morita Antiques (Aoyama)

Aoyama Kotto Dori (Aoyama antique street) connects Minami-Aoyama Go chome crossing on Aoyama Dori to Roppongi Dori. The name is derived from the cluster of antique shops that opened there after the Pacific War. There are now more office buildings and boutiques, and the former shops have become high-rises except for a select few. "Morita Antiques" is one of the survivors. Its long history dates back to 1965 when it started as an antique craft shop, but now mostly sells old or dyed fabrics. The shop also has a collection of items that were dyed by hand in Southeast Asia, China, or Turkey, which are all origins of Japanese dyeing methods. There are many exquisite pieces, each collected on location, and delightful antique pieces that not only collectors, but anyone would want to hold and cherish. Old fabrics such as Futons and Kimonos can be framed and decorated as art or be used as table runners. "The beauty of old fabrics is that they produce a softer texture with use over time. Please take a look and feel the fabric."

(H) 10:00-19:00 (T) 03-3407-4466 (C) N/A (Ad) 1st floor Kurasawa bldg, 5-12-2 Minami-Aoyama, Minato-ku (Ac) 6-min walk from Omotesando Station (Toei Line) (U) www.morita-antiques.com

㉑ 杂货店“蓝与白”（麻布十番）

出生于美国的蓝染研究专家埃米·加藤于1975年成立了“蓝与白”。正如其名，店内摆放的布类小物及杂货，也大多是蓝色或白色，从视觉上为人们营造了一个蓝与白的世界。店主埃米是古布收藏家，尤其喜欢蓝染。古布、蓝染工艺的绳子、丝线等藏品摆放随意而自然，别具一番风味。店内不仅有二手的古布和相关饰物，还有现代手艺匠人用日本传统技术制作的作品，以及将古老的材料重新加工后的作品。这些作品对于“日式”的重新定义，同样给日本人带来了新鲜感。埃米在美国出版了数本介绍日本室内设计的书籍，店内也有许多外国的顾客。这里有许多设计时尚却又饱含日式风格的作品，适合喜欢日本现代手工艺品的顾客。在这里还可以买到毛巾、器皿等日常生活用品。

（时）11:00—18:00 （电）03-3451-0537 （休）年末年初 （址）港区麻布十番2-9-2 2层 （交）地铁麻布十番站步行5分钟 （网）blueandwhitetokyo.com

㉑ BLUE&WHITE (Azabu-juban)

This shop was started in 1975 by indigo dyeing researcher Amy Kato, who was born in the United States. As its name suggests, the shop has a precious display of indigo and white items, with small indigo-dyed items and general merchandise creating a world of blue & white colors. Since Amy is also a collector of old indigo fabric, it is worth glancing at her private collection of BORO, indigo-dyed robes and threads subtly displayed in the shop. It is a unique collection of not just old items, but also a thoughtful selection of pieces created by modern artists using traditional Japanese techniques as well as items repurposed from old material. These new Japanese concepts are refreshing even for Japanese people. The shop is also frequented by tourists from abroad, partly as Amy has published several books in America on Japanese interior decorating. Many of the items are modern designs with a Japanese feel, making it a perfect place to find a "contemporary" gift from Japan. The shop also sells everyday items such as washcloths and utsuwa.

(H) 11:00-18:00 (T) 03-3451-0537 (C) New Year's holidays (Ad) 2nd floor, 2-9-2 Azabu-juban, Minato-ku (Ac) 5-min walk from Azabu-juban Station (Toei Line) (U) blueandwhitetokyo.com

去古布博物馆，看一场与众不同的展览

A MUSEUM OF BORO WITH UNIQUE EXHIBITIONS

日本艺人经纪公司 AMUSE 于 2009 年在东京浅草开办了一家以布文化和浮世绘为主题的博物馆。馆内陈列着已故日本民俗学者田中忠三郎历经 50 年收集的普通人的衣物以及生活用品等，藏品共 3 万件，从中甄选了 1 500 件进行陈列展示。馆内的常设展览有古布展、生活用品展等。除此之外，还展出过黑泽明导演的电影《梦》中使用的衣服、展板等。博物馆经常会设定不同的主题，从数量庞大的藏品中挑选藏品进行展览，还有浮世绘剧场等。观展时如同漫游在日本文化的海洋中，让人获得充实感。

This is a museum of fabrics and *Ukiyo-E* (Japanese woodblock prints), which opened in 2009 in Asakusa, Tokyo, and was created by Amuse, a Japanese entertainment company. It exhibits 1,500 of the 30,000 pieces of BORO civilian clothes and other items such as general merchandise that the late folklorist, Chuzaburo Tanaka, collected 50 years. There is a permanent exhibit for BORO and Japanese folk articles, as well as specially themed exhibits such as a vast collection of costumes and storyboards used in director Akira Kurosawa's film, *Dreams*, and has an Ukiyo-E theater to fully experience Japanese culture.

AMUSE 博物馆（浅草）

(时)10:00—18:00 (电)03-5806-1181（馆长）(休)星期一（若星期一是节假日则顺延到星期二）(费)1 080 日元 (址)台东区浅草 2-34-3 (交)东京地铁银座线浅草站步行 5 分钟，东京都营浅草线浅草站步行 8 分钟 (网)www.amusemuseum.com

AMUSE MUSEUM (Asakusa)

(H) 10:00-18:00 (T) 03-5806-1181 (main) (C) Monday (or Tuesday, if Monday is a national holiday) (F) ¥1,080 (Ad) 2-34-3 Asakusa, Taito-ku (Ac) 8-min walk from Asakusa Station (Toei Line) (U) www.amusemuseum.com

馆内展示的是默默无闻的手工艺人或妇女手织的古布。经过缝缝补补的古布是完整的艺术品。馆内的陈列方式能将古布的细节都呈现出来，可以一件一件地仔细观赏。

Fabrics made by unknown craftspeople and women are exhibited in the museum. BORO, made by patching many pieces of fabric together, becomes one complete piece of art. They are exhibited to allow all details to be observed piece by piece.

馆内独特的陈列方式，或展现古布的褪色程度，或展现其柔软质地。一层是店铺，主题是“日式”。二层及以上几层则是陈列室。六层有一间酒吧，可以望到浅草寺，视角独好。

It is a unique exhibition that shows how the colors have faded and fabric has softened from repeated use over time. The 1st floor is a Japanese-themed souvenir shop. The 2nd floor and above are exhibition galleries. There is a bar on the 6th floor with a spectacular view of Sensoji Temple.

和服

和服是日本民族服饰，有独特的文化特征，在古董中也是较贴近日常生活的门类。和服的制作年代各异且材质多种多样，因此建议根据实际用途来寻找。但是，因为以前日本人个头较矮小，所以现在的年轻人穿起来可能略显短小。因此，实际试穿一下确认码数就显得尤为重要。另外，在购买二手和服时还要注意检查是否有污垢或虫洞。

KIMONO

Kimono is one of the hallmarks of Japanese culture and is relatively well known in the world of antiques. Since its history spans across many decades and is made using a large variety of materials, it is recommended to find one based on the purpose. Japanese people were shorter in the old days, so Kimonos are sometimes too short for the younger westernized generation. It is important to try them on to find the right size. They should also be checked for stains and moth holes.

古布

古布指的是古代平民百姓平时穿的衣服或在破损的寝具上缝补的带有补丁的布。古布体现了对布的爱惜。除此之外，布的柔软质地以及补丁与布的搭配也产生了美感，所以现在人们已经将古布看作一个艺术领域了。尽管日本东北地区及北陆地区的农民、渔民对布非常爱惜，但经过多次使用后最终还是扔掉了。现在，收藏家收集古布非常困难，他们费尽心思收集起来的古布大多用来展览或售卖。古布在海外也极受欢迎。

BORO

It is a type of fabric such as Noragi or gowns worn by civilians, that have become frazzled with "wear and tear," and have been mended with patchwork. Since it encouraged the importance of fabric, and its soft texture and beauty of its patchwork became newly recognized, it was established as a new genre of art called "BORO." While farmers and fishermen in the Tohoku and Hokuriku areas take good care of them, they still tend to be thrown away in the end, so BORO that are sold or used in exhibitions often require a lot of effort by collectors to find and gather them in quantities. They are also highly popular abroad.

古董集市

东京古董集市名录
LIST OF ANTIQUE MARKETS IN TOKYO

Japanese Antique Market

露天古董集市（有明）

于东京国际展览中心举办。
聚集日本 500 家古董商店。日本参展店铺最多的古董集市。

(时) 每年举办两次，各举办 3 天，开放时间为 10:00—17:00 (电)无 (费)1 000 日元（仅限当日使用）(址) 江东区有明 3-11-1 东京国际展览中心 (交)JR 临海线国际展览中心站步行 7 分钟 (网) www.kottoh-jamboree.com

ANTIQUE JAMBOREE (Ariake)

Japan's largest antique market with 500 businesses from all over Japan.

(H)Open twice a year for 3 days per market, 10:00-17:00 (T)N/A (F)¥1,000 (same-day ticket) (Ad) Tokyo big Site, 3-11-1 Ariake, Koto-ku (Ac) 7-min walk from Kokusai Tenjijo Station (JR Line) (U)www.kottoh-jamboree.com

---

藏品跳蚤市场、废品艺术展（竹桥）

主营 20 世纪 50 至 80 年代的古器物、收藏品，
还有充满昭和时代韵味的杂货。

(时)每年举办三次，各举办 2 天，开放时间为 11:00—17:00 (电)无 (费)1 000 日元 (址) 千代田区北之丸公园 2-1 科技馆 (交)东京地铁竹桥站步行 5 分钟 (网)www.toyshow.co.jp

COLLECTABLE FLEA MARKET (Takebashi)

A flea market of vintages and collectibles from the 1950s to 1980s.

(H) Open 3 times a year for 2 days per market, 11:00-17:00 (T)N/A (F)¥1,000 (Ad) Tokyo Science Museum, 2-1 Kitanomarukoen, Chiyoda-ku (Ac) 5-min walk from Takebashi Station (Tokyo Metro Line) (U) www.toyshow.co.jp

---

世田谷古布集市（世田谷）

始于 1578 年的传统集市。从古董店到旧书店，
约 700 家店铺参展。还有特产“代宫饼”，值得品尝！

(时)12 月 15 日—16 日、1 月 15 日—16 日举办，开放时间为 9:00—20:00 (电)03-5432-3333 (费)免费 (址)世田谷站与上町站之间 (交)东急世田谷线世田谷站步行 3 分钟 (网)www.city.setagaya.lg.jp/setagaya/11000/11004/d00125000.html

SETAGAYA BOROICHI (Setagaya)

Traditional event that started in 1578 with 700 stalls from old books to antiques.

(H)December 15-16, January 15-16, 9:00-20:00 (T)03-5432-3333 (F)N/A (Ad)Between Setagaya Station and Uemachi Station (Ac) 3-min walk from Setagaya Station (Tokyu Line) (U) www.city.setagaya.lg.jp/setagaya/11000/11004/d00125000.html

古董集市

东京古董集市名录
LIST OF ANTIQUE MARKETS IN TOKYO

Japanese Antique Market

有明跳蚤市场（有明）

集聚杂货、家具、古衣物、玩具等古藏品与古玩。
与其他国家相同，采用在车上摆放、售卖的形式。

(时)每月 1 次，星期日举办，开放时间为 10:00—17:00 (电)045-681-5856 (费)免费 (址)江东区有明 3-7-26 East Promenade 广场，国际展览中心前 (交)临海线国际展览中心站步行 1 分钟 (网) www.mihonichi.com/ariakeretro.html

ARIAKE RETRO FLEA MARKET (Ariake)

Vintage and antique general merchandise, furniture, clothes, and toys.

(H)Once a month on Sundays, 10:00-17:00 (T)045-681-5856 (F)N/A (Ad) Ariake East Promenade Square in front of Tokyo Big Sight, 3-7-26 Ariake, Koto-ku (Ac)1-min walk from Kokusai Tenjijo Station (U)www.mihonichi.com/ariakeretro.html

---

浅草古今和服集市（浅草）

经过精挑细选的全国各地和服商家参展，
从古和服到腰带、古布、和服小饰物等，应有尽有。

(时)每年举办 1 次，为期 2 天，开放时间为 11:00—18:00 (电)无 (费)免费 (址)台东区浅草桥 1-22-16 浅草桥大厦 2 层 (交)JR 总武线浅草桥站步行 1 分钟 (网) www.kottou-roman.jp/kimono

ASAKUSA KONJAKU KIMONO DAIICHI (Asakusa)

Kimono companies from all over Japan selling antique Kimono, Obi, and fabric.

(H) Open once a year for 2 days per market, 11:00-18:00 (T) N/A (F) N/A (Ad) 2F Asakusa Hulic Hall, 1-22-16 Asakusabashi, Taito-ku (Ac) 1-min walk from Asakusabashi Station (JR Line) (U) www.kottou-roman.jp/kimono

---

西荻古董节（西荻洼）

古民居井荻会馆中挤满 20 多个展位。
门前、房间内古董遍布。

(时)4 月、10 月的第 2 个周六举办，开放时间为 9:30—17:00 (电)03-3397-8737 (费)免费 (址)杉并区西荻北 4-35-9 井荻会馆 (交)JR 中央线西荻洼站步行 10 分钟 (网)www.kottosuki.com

NISHIOGI ANTIQUE FESTIVAL (Nishiogikubo)

A market with 20 stalls held at an folk house called "Iogi Kaikan."

(H) Open 2nd Saturdays of April and October, 9:30-17:00 (T) 03-3397-8737 (F) N/A (Ad) Iogi Kaikan, 4-35-9 Nishiogikita, Suginami-ku (Ac)10-min walk from Nishiogikubo Station (JR Line) (U) www.kottosuki.com

古董集市

东京古董集市名录
LIST OF ANTIQUE MARKETS IN TOKYO

Japanese Antique Market

花园神社古董集市（新宿）

每周日，在花园神社内举办的古董集市。
花园神庄地处新宿正中心，游客络绎不绝。

(时)星期日（需要提前确认），开放时间为 6:00 到日落 (电)无 (费)免费 (址)新宿区新宿 5-17-3 花园神社 (交)地铁丸之内线新宿三丁目站步行 3 分钟 (网) www.kottou-ichi.jp

HANAZONO JINJA AOZORA ANTIQUE MARKET (Shinjuku)

An antique market held at the Hanazono Jinja (Shinto shrine) every Sunday.

(H)Open every Sunday(Please call to check), 6:00-dusk (T)N/A (F)N/A (Ad)Hanazono Shrine, 5-17-3 Shinjuku, Shinjuku-ku (Ac)3-min walk from Shinjuku Sanchome Station (Toie Line) (U)www.kottou-ichi.jp

---

高幡不动 Gozare 古董集市（高幡不动）

在坐落着五重塔的寺院内举办的集市。
从古器物到古玩，应有尽有。

(时)每月第 3 个星期日举办，开放时间为 7:00—16:00 (电)090-3314-1994 (费)免费 (址)日野市高幡 733 高幡不动 (交)京王线高幡不动站步行 2 分钟 (网) www.kottouichi.jp/takahata.htm

TAKAHATA FUDO GOZARE MARKET (Takahata Fudo)

Antique fair held near the Goju-no-to pagoda at Takahata Fudo-son Temple.

(H) 3rd Sunday of every month, 7:00-16:00 (T) 090-3314-1994 (F) N/A (Ad) Takahata Fudo, 733 Takahata, Hino-shi (Ac)2-min walk from Takahata Fudo Station (Keio Line) (U) www.kottouichi.jp/takahata.htm

---

护国寺古董集市（护国寺）

在护国寺内售卖古董、日用品，
还有二手相机、盆栽、饰品。

(时)每月第 2 个星期六，开放时间为 7:00—15:00 (电)080-3697-9790 (费)免费 (址)文京区大塚 5-40-1 护国寺 (交)东京地铁有乐町线护国寺站出站即是 (网)www.geocities.jp/gokokuji_kottouichi

GOKOKUJI TEMPLE ANTIQUE MARKET (Gokokuji)

Outdoor booths selling antiques and everyday items at Gokokuji Temple.

(H)Open 2nd Saturday of every month, 7:00-15:00 (T)080-3697-9790 (F)N/A (Ad)Gokokiuji Temple, 5-40-1 Otsuka, Bunkyo-ku, Tokyo (Ac)0-min walk from Gokokuji Station (Tokyo Metro Line) (U)www.geocities.jp/gokokuji_kottouichi

东京古董集市名录
LIST OF ANTIQUE MARKETS IN TOKYO

新宿古玩展（新宿）

从日本古董到西方古玩，品类丰富。
商品价格每日均有浮动，实惠的每日特价商品备受关注。

(时)每年2次，每次举办3天，开放时间为11:00—18:00（最后一天到17:00）(电)无 (费)免费 (址)新宿区西新宿2-7-1小田急第一生命大楼 (交)地铁大江户线都厅前站步行2分钟 (网)www.antique-stage.com

ANTIQUE FAIR IN SHINJUKU (Shinjuku)

Sells a variety of wakotto and Western antiques and has deals that change daily.

(H)Opens twice a year for 3 days per market, 11:00-18:00 (ends at 17:00 on the last day) (T) N/A (F) N/A (Ad)Odakyu Daiichi Seimei Bldg., 2-7-1 Nishi-shinjuku, Shinjuku-ku (Ac)2-min walk from Tochomae Station (Toei Line) (U) www.antique-stage.com

ARK Hills 赤坂跳蚤市场（赤坂）

商店包括杂货、二手衣物、珠宝等，门类齐全。
还有美食摊、现场演唱会，可以享受一整天。

(时)每月第4个星期日，开放时间为11:00—17:00 (电)03-6406-6663 (费)免费 (址)港区赤坂1-12-32 ARK Hills卡拉扬广场 (交)东京地铁南北线六本木一丁目站步行1分钟 (网)www.facebook.com/AKASAKA.NOMINOICHI

AKASAKA ANTIQUE FAIR IN ARK HILLS (Akasaka)

Sells second-hand clothes and jewelry, and there are food stalls and live bands.

(H)Open every 4th Sunday, 11:00-17:00 (T) 03-6406-6663 (F) N/A (Ad) Ark Karajan Square, Ark Hills, 1-12-32 Akasaka, Minato-ku (Ac)1-min walk from Roppongi I-chome Station (Tokyo Metro Line) (U) www.facebook.com/AKASAKA.NOMINOICHI

大和 promenade 古董集市（大和）

日本首屈一指的大型露天古董集市，让人想从东京出发，前去一探究竟。
每次都会有300多家店铺参展，可以淘到物美价廉的宝贝。

(时)每月第3个星期六，开放时间为5:00—16:00 (电)无 (费)免费 (址)神奈川县大和市大和站东西步道 (交)小田急江之岛线大和站直达 (网)www.yamato-kottouichi.jp

YAMATO PROMENADE ANTIQUE MARKET (Yamato)

Largest outdoor antique market with more than 300 stalls and great bargains.

(H)Open every 3rd Saturday, 5:00-16:00 (T)N/A (F)N/A (Ad)Eastwest promenade at Yamato Station, Yamato-shi, Kanagawa (Ac) Yamato Station (Odakyu Line) (U) www.yamato-kottouichi.jp

小百科 / GLOSSARY

伊万里烧：即伊万里瓷器，江户时代会从伊万里地区的港口出口瓷器（多为有田烧），如今从这里出口的瓷器都被称为“伊万里瓷器”。江户时代烧制的则被称为“古伊万里瓷器”。

日本六大古窑：越前古窑、濑户古窑、常滑古窑、备前古窑、信乐古窑、丹波古窑。

常滑烧：窑址位于爱知县知多半岛西海岸常滑市。其烧制历史可以追溯到千年前。镰仓时代（1185—1333 年）开始生产朴素且坚固的日用杂器，起初不用釉料，多使用被称为“自然釉”烧制法。到了江户时代（1603—1868 年），人们利用当地陶土含铁量多的特点烧制出了朱泥烧、白泥烧、火色烧等陶制品，也奠定了日本现代陶制品的基础。

备前烧：日本六大古窑之一，窑址位于冈山县备前市。备前烧的特色在于不上釉、不绘彩，完全靠火和技巧来制作陶器，十分考验技术。

有田烧：是以日本佐贺县有田町为中心出产的瓷器。日本三大名烧之一。在江户时代后期日本各地开始瓷器生产之前，有田是日本唯一长期出产瓷器的地方。有田烧按制造时期、样式，大体分为初期伊万里、古九谷、柿右卫门、金兰手等。还有贡皇室用品称为“禁里样式”。

美浓烧：日本美浓地区（现在的岐阜县）因为拥有丰富的陶瓷原料——粘土，所以自古出产陶瓷制品。美浓烧的作品比较常见，适合日常生活使用。

九谷烧：日本三大名烧之一，历史悠久。九谷烧的作品颜色较为艳丽且多采用手工彩绘、染绘的技法，釉色艳丽。

京烧：也称清水烧。清水烧起始于公元 5 世纪后半期，因起始的窑口位于清水寺门前，所以被命名为清水烧。清水烧具有表现手法多样、釉色丰富、画法细腻的特点。

唐津烧：唐津烧的窑址遍布于日本佐贺县的北半部，还有长崎县的部分地区（古时为肥前国），唐津烧是这些窑的总称，地处九州西北部，面朝唐津湾。据说在奈良时期，这里是中国唐代派船入日的要津，唐津其名的来源可能与此有关。17 世纪后，以鬼子岳（岸岳）山麓为中心的诸窑产品，都由唐津港运出，故称唐津烧。

NOTES

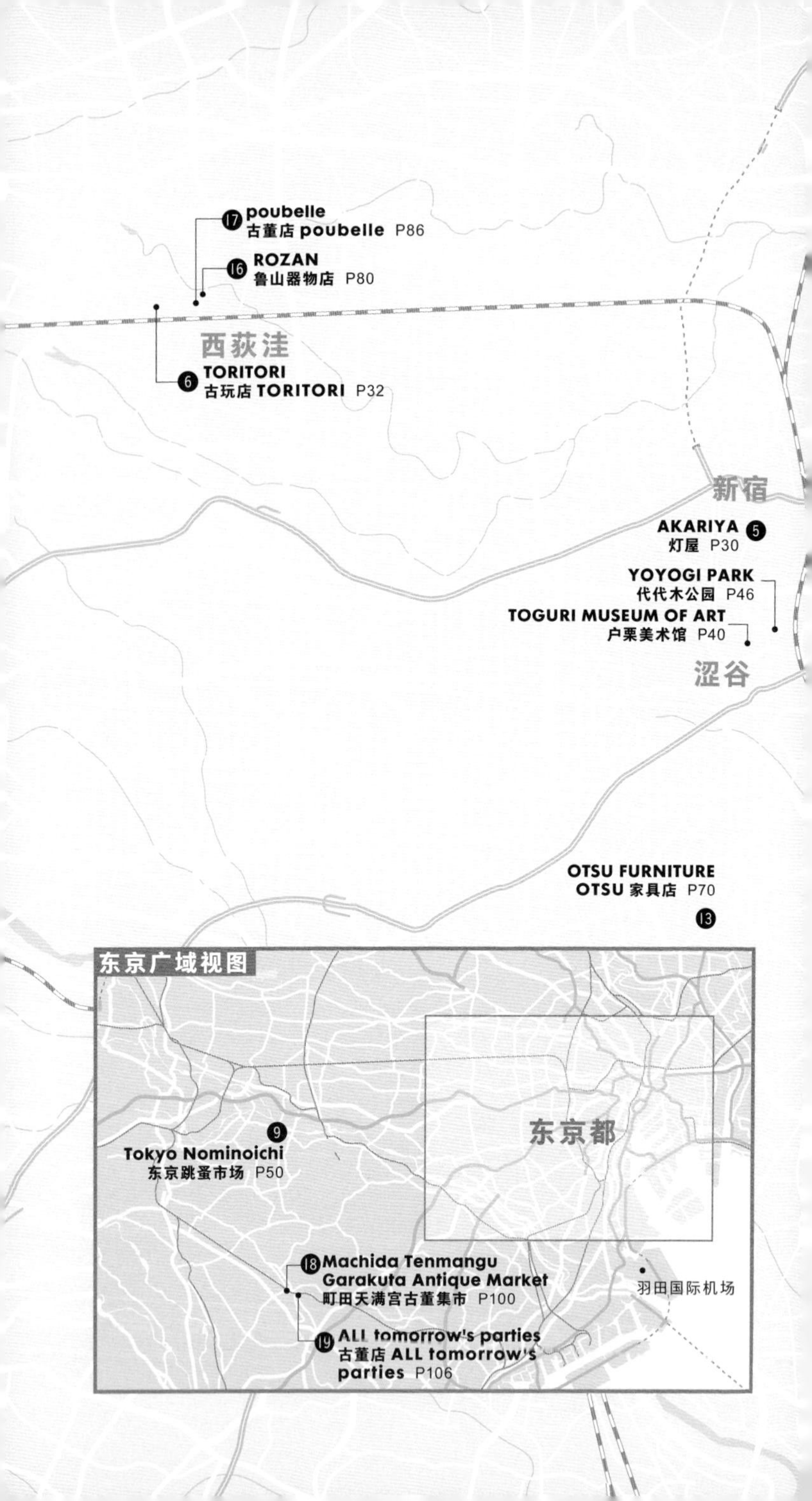

poubelle
古董店 poubelle P86
ROZAN
鲁山器物店 P80
西荻洼
TORITORI
古玩店 TORITORI P32
新宿
AKARIYA
灯屋 P30
YOYOGI PARK
代代木公园 P46
TOGURI MUSEUM OF ART
户栗美术馆 P40
涩谷
OTSU FURNITURE
OTSU 家具店 P70
东京广域视图
东京都
Tokyo Nominoichi
东京跳蚤市场 P50
Machida Tenmangu
Garakuta Antique Market
町田天满宫古董集市 P100
羽田国际机场
ALL tomorrow's parties
古董店 ALL tomorrow's
parties P106

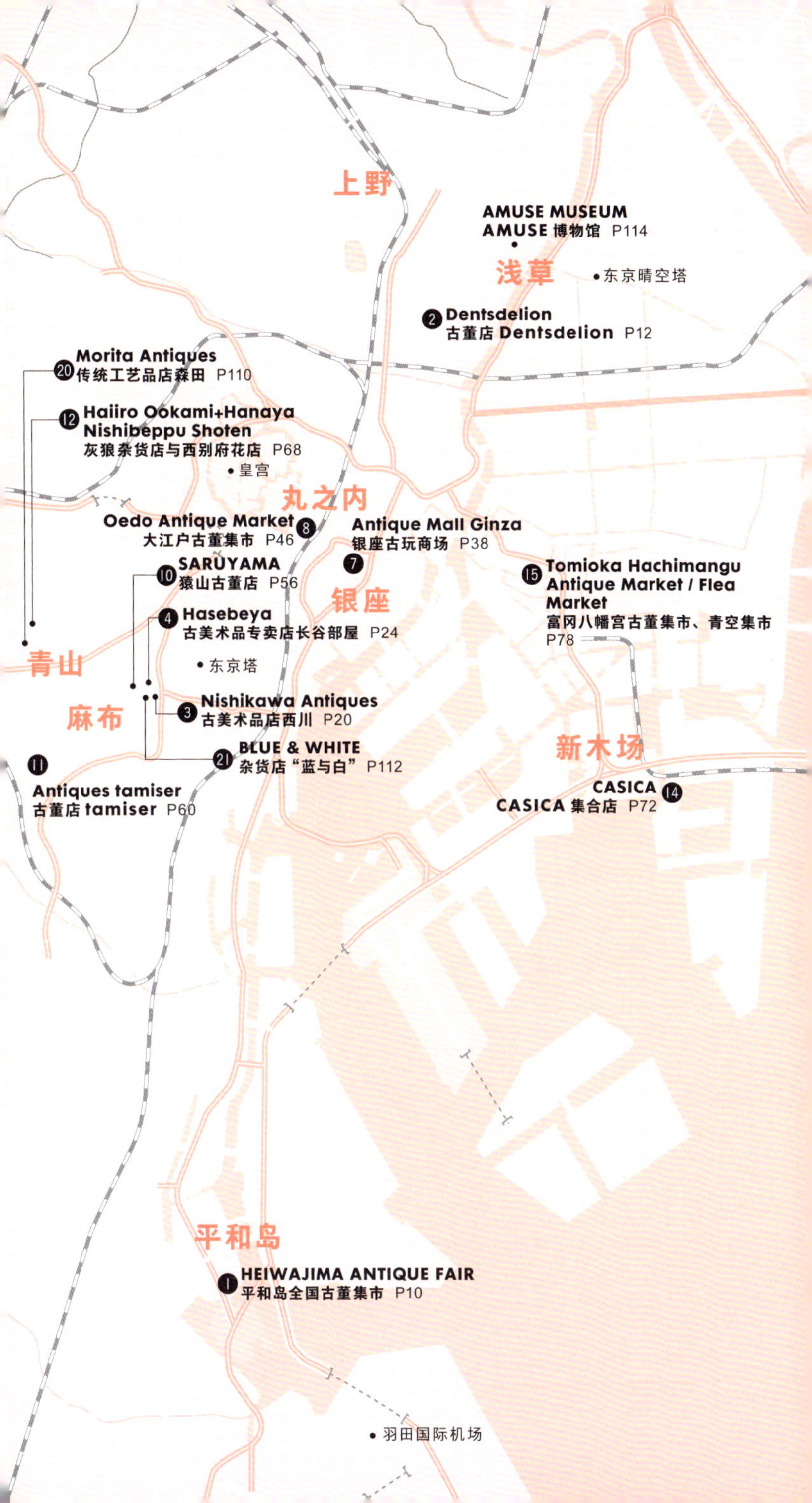

上野
AMUSE MUSEUM
AMUSE 博物馆 P114
浅草
东京晴空塔
2 Dentsdelion
古董店 Dentsdelion P12
20 Morita Antiques
传统工艺品店森田 P110
12 Haiiro Ookami+Hanaya Nishibeppu Shoten
灰狼杂货店与西别府花店 P68
皇宫
丸之内
Oedo Antique Market 8
大江户古董集市 P46
Antique Mall Ginza
银座古玩商场 P38
7
15 Tomioka Hachimangu Antique Market / Flea Market
富冈八幡宫古董集市、青空集市 P78
10 SARUYAMA
猿山古董店 P56
银座
4 Hasebeya
古美术品专卖店长谷部屋 P24
青山
东京塔
3 Nishikawa Antiques
古美术品店西川 P20
麻布
新木场
21 BLUE & WHITE
杂货店“蓝与白” P112
11
Antiques tamiser
古董店 tamiser P60
CASICA 14
CASICA 集合店 P72
平和岛
1 HEIWAJIMA ANTIQUE FAIR
平和岛全国古董集市 P10
羽田国际机场

Original Japanese edition published by Bijutsu Shuppan-Sha Co., Ltd., Tokyo.
This Simplified Chinese language edition is published by arrangement with Bijutsu Shuppan-Sha Co., Ltd., Tokyo in care of CITIC PRESS JAPAN CO., LTD, Tokyo

本书仅限中国大陆地区发行销售

日文版工作人员

Cover Illustration: NORITAKE　Designer: TUESDAY (Tomohiro+Chiyo Togawa)
Map: Manami Yamamoto (DIG.Factory)
Photographer: Suguru Ariga (except p10-11, 38-41, 46-53, 68-73, 78-79, 86-89, 114-115)
Japanese Writer: Motoko Sasaki　Translator: Kinue Lee
Proofreader (Japanese): Mine Kobo　Proofreader (English): Jonathan Berry
Editorial Director: Miki Usui (BIJUTSU SHUPPAN-SHA CO., LTD.)

图书在版编目（CIP）数据

日本古董 / 日本美术出版社书籍编辑部编著；崔倩倩译. -- 北京：中信出版社，2019.7（2019.9 重印）
（东京艺术之旅）
ISBN 978-7-5217-0419-8

Ⅰ. ①日… Ⅱ. ①日… ②崔… Ⅲ. ①历史文物－介绍－日本 Ⅳ. ① K883.13

中国版本图书馆 CIP 数据核字 (2019) 第 073287 号

日本古董

编　　著：【日】美术出版社书籍编辑部
译　　者：崔倩倩
出版发行：中信出版集团股份有限公司
（北京市朝阳区惠新东街甲4号富盛大厦2座　邮编　100029）
承 印 者：北京雅昌艺术印刷有限公司

开　　本：880mm × 1230mm　1/32　　印　　张：4
字　　数：67千字　　版　　次：2019年7月第1版
印　　次：2019年9月第4次印刷　　京权图字：01-2019-2332
广告经营许可证：京朝工商广字第8087号
书　　号：ISBN 978-7-5217-0419-8
定　　价：45.00元